D0949097

UNDERSTANDING

UNDERSTANDING

Eliminating Stress
and Finding Serenity
in Life and Relationships

SECOND EDITION, REVISED

Jane Nelsen, Ed.D.

PRIMA PUBLISHING

PRIMA PUBLISHING and colophon are registered trademarks of Prima Communications, Inc.

Library of Congress Cataloging-in-Publication Data

Nelsen, Jane.
　　Understanding : eliminating stress and finding serenity in life and relationships / Jane Nelsen.—Rev. 2nd ed.
　　　　p.　cm.
　　Includes bibliographical references and index.
　　ISBN　0-7615-0559-8
　　1. Peace of mind. 2. Happiness. 3. Interpersonal relations.
4. Stress (Psychology)—Prevention.　I. Title.
BF637.P3N45　　1996
158' .1—dc20　　　　　　　　　　　　　　　　　　　　96-31337
　　　　　　　　　　　　　　　　　　　　　　　　　　　　　CIP
96 97 98 99 00 HH 10 9 8 7 6 5 4 3 2 1
　　Printed in the United States of America

How to Order:

　　Single copies may be ordered from Prima Publishing, P.O. Box 1260BK, Rocklin, CA 95677; telephone (916) 632-4400. Quantity discounts are also available. On your letterhead, include information concerning the intended use of the books and the number of books you wish to purchase.

Visit us online at http://www.primapublishing.com

Praise for *Understanding*

"This is a warm and wonderfully written book which will help people find understanding and compassion in their relationships with children, spouses, employers, friends—and most importantly, themselves."

Kimberly Kiddoo, Ph.D.
psychologist, Coral Gables, Florida

"Reading *Understanding* has assisted many of my patients to access that transcendent intelligence from which insight and wisdom emanate. With humility, clarity, and joy, Dr. Nelsen points to this potential within all of us."

William F. Pettit, M.D.
board-certified psychiatrist, Aberdeen, South Dakota

"The reason I recommend *Understanding* so highly to all of my friends and students is that it gives us effective tools for staying on course toward real joy in our lives. The revised edition is better than ever."

Max Skousen
author of more than twenty-five books, national lecturer on management methods and economics, and the developer and teacher of the course, "The Hidden Key to Peace"

"To say that the principles in this book have completely changed how I live my life is an understatement. I appreciate Jane's simple way of helping me find an *understanding* that integrates every aspect of my life: spiritual seeker, wife, mom, and therapist. I have finally found the perfect marriage of spirituality and psychology."

Jean Traughber-Seymour
licensed M.F.C.C., San Diego, California

"Jane Nelsen's clearly laid out wisdom makes it easy to understand the depths of consciousness while ascending to the heights of awareness. All who are interested in mastering their moods and expressing their full potential of love and happiness will benefit from this insightful guide."

Valerie Seeman Moreton, N.D.
author of Heal the Cause: Creating
Wellness—Body, Mind and Spirit

"Gratitude! This is the best one-word description that I and many of my students have used after reading *Understanding*. As a twenty-five-year veteran of teaching and counseling, I have found that the simple wisdom expressed by Dr. Nelsen can convey what I am unable to accomplish through countless lectures. Thank you Jane; you keep me laughing, hoping, and growing."

Bill Call, Ed.D
*licensed marital and family therapist
and counselor, Tulsa, Oklahoma*

"Just let go, trust, and allow your peace of mind to come from within. The truth that sets us free really can be that simple. Jane Nelsen has written of this natural process, which is inherent within all of us, in such an understandable manner. A terrific book to carry around with you."

Bill Hutcherson, Ph.D.
psychologist, Roseville, California

Contents

Contents

Foreword

It is not an exaggeration to say that the first edition of *Understanding* changed my life, and consequently the lives of literally hundreds of my clients and students over the last several years. When I first was introduced to this book, I had been teaching and counseling for many years. I believed I was a successful therapist when I helped my clients learn to "cope" with their problems. After all, I was pretty good at "coping" myself.

Understanding threw me into my heart where my own healing continued like I would never have imagined possible. I have found this true for many of the people that I have counseled and taught since that time. I have suggested to my clients that one can't read *Understanding* just once or twice. It is a lifetime process of struggling to stay in the *heart*. This book, written for the layman, takes me back into my heart every time I read it. I have reviewed this revision several times, and can say with complete honesty that it is better than ever in achieving this end.

The science of Psychology of Mind evolved out of the 1980s. The followers seemed to be a strange mix of mystics and board-certified psychologists. After thoroughly digesting Dr. Nelsen's book, my enthusiasm and personal results from her work drove me to send for and study in depth all of the material I could get my hands on that explained this new science. I soon discovered that there is nothing out there for the ordinary person that comes close to explaining the principles and precepts of this remarkable science as does *Understanding*.

We seem to have an imbalance leaning toward the "head" in our culture, which makes it very difficult to find lasting joy and satisfaction in all of our relationships. The programmed thought system generates our mental, and most of our physical, ills. It is not easy for those of us who were raised in our thought-dominated culture to grasp the concept of being able to stand back objectively and view how the brain works. "Not able to see the forest for the trees" is more than just a cliché when it comes to trying to understand ourselves and why we *think* and thus act the way we do. *Understanding,* in my experience, helps create this new awareness as nothing else in literature is able to do.

I have found that understanding my dsyfunction in relationships with myself and others is, however, only part of the healing equation. There are many practitioners and hoards of books on the market right now that do a wonderful job of helping us see where our emotional problems came from. I agree with Dr. Nelsen that some of this information can be extremely helpful. These excellent works can open the doors for personal growth when used to help people heal old beliefs from the past that block them from accessing their hearts, their inner wisdom, their spiritual source. However, after years of experience, I have found that for a complete life change—a rebirth, if you will—to take place in a person's life, something more than just getting in touch with the reasons for his or her dysfunction needs to occur. This is where the principles taught in *Understanding* have had such great impact.

In clear, precise, understandable dialogue, Dr. Nelsen is able to make it easy to get out of the thought system, which creates all dysfunction, and into the heart where real emotional and behavioral change can begin to take place. Rereading the chapters creates this change effortlessly.

Especially helpful are the later chapters which contain clear, realistic life experience examples where changing the heart can change the outcomes of previous relationship breakdowns. It seems that emotions are some of the most misunderstood and feared of all constructs within the field of psychology. Understanding that emotions are created instantaneously from feelings, and learning that I have control over my feelings is one of the greatest breakthroughs in the study of "mind" in the twentieth century. My feelings are totally different when I am in my heart than when I am in my programmed thought system.

A well-known actor recently stated publicly that self-help books had changed his life, and that he lived on a steady diet of them. I can personally understand why he could make such a remark. People who are seeking to grow and who are willing to pay the price for that growth will eventually find the way. However, as I have often told my seminar students, you could take away every book I have but one, Jane Nelsen's *Understanding,* and I could still maintain my own emotional health and love of life. I share with them the honest fact that the equation for personal happiness and contentment in my own life shifted dramatically from a twenty percent happy, eighty percent coping state, to a realistic ninety percent happy, ten percent coping state, simply from being introduced to her book many years ago.

Someone said once, "If we continue to do what we've always done, we'll always get what we've always got." Our culture has always enthroned the head or intellect as our master and doggedly insisted on trying to solve all of our problems with it, not realizing that it *is* the problem. My great hope and dream for the future of mental health in our world is that with renewed "understanding" we can do something different and thus start reaping better emotional rewards—in other words, "change our *hearts.*" This book is more than just a start, it is the very *way.*

MERRILL J. BAILEY M.ED.

Acknowledgments

I was once a workshop junkie. I used to wonder in jest if I would ever find the last workshop—one that would finally teach me the magic techniques that would give me enough competence and confidence to be truly helpful to myself and others. I never found what I was looking for. Instead, I found something better—principles that taught me where competence, confidence, and wisdom are and always have been— within myself. I had read and heard, over and over, the advice to go within, but I didn't know how to do it.

The intellectual knowledge that "the kingdom of heaven is within," and "as a man thinketh, so is he" was not new to me, but I had never experienced these truths. I finally discovered a seminar where principles were explained that led me to experience my inner kingdom of happiness and peace of mind. I gratefully acknowledge and give thanks to George Pransky and Robert Kausen, who put up with my "what-ifs" and "yes, buts" until I was finally able to hear at a deeper level.

After experiencing such dramatic results in my life from what I learned from George Pransky and Robert Kausen, I felt inspired to spend six months in fellowship at the Advanced Human Studies Institute in Coral Gables, Florida. Studying and working with Dr. Rick Suarez and Dr. Kimberly Kiddoo was truly a beautiful and enriching experience. What a privilege to be led to a deeper understanding of inner resources via the wisdom of these pioneers and innovators of the Psychology of Mind.

I originally intended to write this book with Kimberly Kiddoo because she was such an inspiration to me. When she decided not to co-author the book she encouraged me to use some of her examples because, as she said, "*Understanding* the examples makes them your own, and getting this out in a book will help so many people." I miss her. Dr. Kiddoo is now in private practice in Coral Gables, Florida.

It is with loving appreciation that I acknowledge Dr. William Pettit, a prominent psychiatrist, who dropped his successful practice and position as a national trainer of a popular growth seminar when he heard the principles of Psychology of Mind. He moved his family to Florida and was finishing his fellowship at the Advanced Human Studies Institute while I was there. I am filled with gratitude as I remember his delightful influence, which is reflected in this book.

It was a special thrill to receive an endorsement from Wayne Dyer. His books and tapes have been an inspiration to me and my family for years. His book, *Gifts from Eykis* (New York: Pocket Books, 1983), is a special gift for those of us who enjoy laughing while we learn profound truths. Wayne continues to inspire me as he "comes out of the closet" with profound spiritual teachings through his new books and lectures.

Because my desire was to be instrumental in helping others experience the joy and serenity found in understanding the principles of Psychology of Mind, it has been a gratifying and humbling experience to hear from so many people who have read the first edition of *Understanding*. That so many would be touched was beyond my comprehension, and I hope that many more will find serenity through this revised edition.

One reason for this revision is the discovery of additional concepts that deepened my level of understanding. This new understanding has led me to revise my belief that one should never go into the past. Thanks to Valerie Seeman Moreton and Max Skousen I learned healing processes for going into the past than helped me heal some beliefs that often blocked my joy and serenity. It now seems like common sense to understand that sometimes we need to heal the beliefs we created as part of our thought systems. Too often these beliefs filter our life experience even when we are not consciously aware of them. Much of this new edition includes information about these healing processes.

The gratitude I feel for Jack and Deborah Bartello is sacred to me. They came into my life immediately after the first edition of *Understanding* was self-published. They have gently introduced me (kicking and screaming all the way) to a beautiful, spiritual world that was unattainable through my thought system. In fact, it is my thought system that did all the kicking and screaming. I recently asked them how they were able to put up with my resistance. They said simply, "There is not any resistance in your energy. We pay more attention to energy than any other communication." Their influence is intricately woven throughout this new edition.

My good friend, Dr. Bill Hutcherson, has been my "workshop junkie" buddy for years. We no longer tolerate the workshops that give validity to the thought system, but still enjoy workshops that take us to our heart and spiritual source. He suggested some deletions in the last edition that I didn't understand until this time. He is ever gentle with his suggestions.

I am especially grateful to my husband, Barry. He is one of the most unconditionally loving people I know. It was the healing of some subconscious beliefs that has allowed me to accept and appreciate his love. Through *understanding* we have learned, even when we get into the dysfunctions of our programmed thought system, to be kind to each other until we learn from the experience or until it passes.

I do not want to give the impression that life is always total bliss. We are on this planet to learn and to grow. Every experience gives us opportunities for learning and growing at whatever depth we choose. All the principles discussed in *Understanding* have helped me view both "good" and "bad" experiences with gratitude—sooner or later. You will understand why after reading this new edition.

My final acknowledgment is to my children, to whom this book is dedicated. We continually love and learn from each other. My daughter Mary made a statement that sums up the value of the principles discussed in this book. I got lost for a short time in feelings of insecurity and was behaving irrationally. Because of *Understanding* it didn't last too long. Mary later said, "I knew you would soon realize what you were doing, Mom."

It is my hope that *Understanding* will help you realize what you are doing, learn from it, and quickly return to your heart, where you will experience joy and serenity.

UNDERSTANDING

1

A Treasure Map

All of us look for answers to help us find happiness and peace of mind. Even though everyone wants this, many find that lasting joy is missing from their lives and relationships. Instead, they live in stress, anxiety, dissatisfaction, disappointment, anger, or depression. The use of anti-depressants, illegal drugs, and alcohol pervades our society, but instead of finding peace of mind, people who rely on drugs find only momentary relief. Many people expect to find happiness through material objects, power, fame, or other people, but they only become addicted to the need for more— more power, fame, relationships, more *things*.

An abundance of wisdom about happiness and peace of mind is available through spoken and written words. You may have experienced inspiration from beautiful words of wisdom and vowed to be better, and then felt disappointed when you did not maintain those inspired feelings. Perhaps you have found that sometimes, even though you remembered what you should do, you just didn't feel able to do it. You may have had times when you felt like giving in to feelings of discouragement, failure, and self-blame. Then you may have felt inspired to do better again—only to repeat the cycle.

How can we remain inspired so that words of wisdom are truly helpful in our lives, instead of remaining mere "shoulds" that we feel we can't live up to? What does it take to understand words of wisdom and integrate them into our being at such a deep level that living in joy and gratitude becomes our normal state of mind? How can we keep to a minimum our lapses from this peaceful state of mind, learn from the situations life presents to us, and return to our natural state of happiness with a deeper understanding of our life purpose?

This book explains four principles of psychological functioning[1] that show you how to access the inner wisdom and happiness you have heard so much about and have probably occasionally experienced. We have all heard that happiness is *within,* but many of us do not understand what that means. We keep looking outside ourselves.

Living in serenity and happiness comes from beautiful feelings inherent within each of us. These natural

---

[1]Originally formulated by Rick Suarez, Ph.D., and Roger C. Mills, Ph.D., *Sanity, Insanity, and Common Sense: The Groundbreaking New Approach to Happiness* (New York: Ballantine, Fawcett Columbine, 1987). Out of print.

good feelings get buried under our programmed thought system. When our inherent good feelings are uncovered, we live naturally in a happy, loving state of being. The kingdom of heaven *is* within.

You may not believe that you have inherent good feelings of joy, wisdom, and peace—or, you may believe it, but feel frustrated that you can't access these feelings. You may feel blocked and imprisoned within your own mind—as indeed you are when you don't understand how a programmed thought system works, and how to get beyond it. An understanding of the four principles can open the prison doors. These principles (discussed in chapters 3 through 6) can serve as a treasure map to *the kingdom of heaven within*. Once you *understand* these principles, you can find the treasures buried deep within you.

Inherent good feelings are like corks in water, naturally bobbing to the surface unless weighted down or buried under debris. Good feelings are natural in human beings, but often they are buried under the debris of negative thoughts taken too seriously (which most of us have become adept at). *Understanding* removes the weights and the debris so that wisdom, gratitude, and peaceful feelings can bob to the top.

Even though happiness, joy, and serenity are inherent within everyone (as will be explained in chapter 3), life presents many lessons for us to learn. Once we understand this, we can be open to the lessons instead of being paralyzed by fear or anxiety or anger when we encounter opportunities to learn. In later chapters, you will learn how to see problems as friends with wonderful life messages. As you learn to recognize this possibility, the fear, anxiety, and anger vanish while the messages remain.

This does not mean we will live in total bliss all of the time. Because of the programmed thought systems we have created (as discussed in chapter 2), it is normal to get hooked into old programming and become lost in our illusions. This is why a treasure map provided by the four principles is such a liberating gift. We can always find our way back home—to our inherent good feelings.

How can I make such claims? Because an understanding of the principles has been such a gift in my own life and in the lives of friends, clients, and other therapists who have come to understand them. Even when we get lost in our thought systems for a while, there is a sense of knowing that we have simply sidetracked ourselves by taking our thoughts seriously. We don't stay sidetracked for long when we understand what we are doing. Being stuck for prolonged periods lets us know that we may need help healing some inaccurate, deeply embedded beliefs. All healing processes are enhanced when based on an understanding of the four principles.

Understanding the principles has increased my understanding of everything and has taken me beyond an intellectual belief in the wonderful words of wisdom I have heard over the years to an *experience* of their meaning. Now, instead of knowing it must be true that the kingdom of heaven is within, I can experience this wonderful state of being anytime I choose to follow the treasure map created by the four principles.

This does not mean I never get off course into unhappiness, but the principles show me exactly how I got off course and point me back in the direction of my inherent good feelings. Like any often-used map, the direction soon becomes so natural that it is easier to find the way without a map. However, just as detours can take us away from a familiar road, we often find ourselves in a detour away from our inherent peace of mind. A programmed thought system is much more complex than a highway system. Ruts and sinkholes (old buried decisions and beliefs) often hook us and lead us astray.

Perhaps we are not truly being led astray; it could be part of a perfect plan that we experience separation from serenity so that we can learn more life lessons. One of the reasons for revising this book is that I have learned to appreciate the value of the lessons and gifts that can be found in my "detours." This decreases my tendency to beat up on myself when my understanding isn't sufficient or permanent.

I'm sure you have noticed that some people get very angry when they have to take a highway detour. Others, however, see detours as an adventure and an opportunity to discover something new. People who don't find the gifts and lessons in their life experiences often stay angry, get depressed, or act like victims. Life becomes a matter of coping instead of a series of occasions of joy and discovery.

Many of us have been well trained in effective coping skills. This can be very helpful, because coping is certainly better than not coping. It brings only temporary relief, however, until the next problem arises. Coping is like bailing water when we don't know how to plug the hole in the boat. (Of course, bailing is much better than sinking.)

The exciting news is that the four basic principles show us how to plug the hole, how to reseal the boat. We don't need to learn how to *cope* with stress or anxiety; we can eliminate them whenever we want to. This book gives many examples of common situations in life and relationships that illustrate how a problem can be eliminated through *understanding*.

Someone once asked, "So, what is the point of all this?"

My answer: "To be happy."

Too many people get caught up in the search for happiness and forget to be happy. I say "forget" because you already know how to be happy, but the knowledge is buried, unused. Buried knowledge is like a well-kept secret.

A client recently said to me, "Well, sure you're happy. Look at all you have."

I replied, "That's the point. I had everything I have now, before I learned about these principles, and I still wasn't happy." I paid more attention to my illusions of insecurity and a false need to prove myself than to my inherent feelings of gratitude, joy, wisdom, and love.

This explains why so many people who have achieved fame, fortune, or other forms of success as defined by our society, are often dissatisfied, whereas others who have little may be quite happy. Happiness has little to do with material possessions or achievements. Lasting happiness and peace of mind are found within, no matter what the circumstances.

In the following poem, Sue Pettit has captured what happens when we listen softly from our hearts:

Coming Home[2]

Coming home to peace and quiet.
Coming home to feelings warm.
Coming home where there's a fullness,
    where love in me is born.
Coming home's a simple journey,
    takes no movement on my part.
Instead of listening to my thoughts,
I listen with
    my heart.

This treasure map to *understanding* is one of the most valuable gifts I have ever received. It has helped me find the buried treasure within myself. It is my hope that it will help you to find lasting peace of mind and happiness within yourself.

Happy treasure hunting!

---

[2]Sue Pettit, *Coming Home,* a book of poems which beautifully and humorously illustrate the four principles of Psychology of Mind. Sunrise Press, Fair Oaks, California (800-456-7770).

2

Listening Softly

As you read this book, listen softly. Listen "from your heart," for insight, for a feeling within that lets you hear truth. In our society, we have been taught to pay more attention to the logic of our intellects than to our hearts. Deepak Chopra suggests another possibility in his book, *The Seven Spiritual Laws of Success:*

> Only the heart knows the correct answer. Most people think the heart is mush and sentimental. But it's not. The heart is intuitive; it's holistic, it's contextual, it's relational. It doesn't have a win-lose orientation. It taps into the cosmic computer—the field of pure potentiality, pure knowledge, and infinite organizing power—and takes everything into account. At times it may not even seem rational, but the heart has a computing ability that is far more accurate and far more

precise than anything within the limits of rational thought.[1]

Listening for an insight from the heart is very different from listening from the intellect.[2] The brain has unlimited capacity and capabilities. However, we have limited our brains with a thought system "programmed" with old decisions based on mistaken interpretations that became solid beliefs which are then seen as reality. This programmed thought system filters any new possibilities, including the truth; it tries to fit everything into what it already knows—or rejects it.

Listen softly for a feeling insight, because words are inadequate to express love, beauty, principle, or any other intangible truth. These truths can be understood only through the personal experience of them, which is beyond words. Someone once asked Louis Armstrong to explain jazz. He replied, "If you can't feel it, I don't know how I can explain it." The only purpose of words in this book is to point you toward the kind of *understanding* you will feel in your heart. If you can't feel it, you will not *understand* it.

We often focus on words and miss the feeling being expressed. Each person hears words from his or her own frame of reference and interpretation. For

---

[1] Deepak Chopra, *The Seven Spiritual Laws of Success* (San Rafael: Amber-Allen Publishing & New World Library, 1994), pp. 43–44.

[2] This is a good definition of what I mean by *understanding*. It is that feeling of inspiration or insight that takes you into the realm of your heart or spiritual source. *Understanding* is a spiritual experience, not an intellectual experience.

example, your mental picture of a dog is different from that of your friends, each of whom loved a different kind of dog. This is why discussions of religion and politics are often avoided; these topics trigger so many differing beliefs and emotions about what is "right" and "wrong" that we stop listening.

Understanding from the heart often can make the traditional definition of words seem topsy-turvy. For example, I once believed forgiveness meant I should do something noble from my intellect. Through *understanding,* forgiveness becomes a nonissue. When I drop my judgments and move into my heart, there is nothing to forgive. Forgiveness feels more like an awareness of the truth about my illusions, or a feeling of compassion, than something to *do.* You will find many examples yourself of how meanings change as you understand the principles.

Listening softly—listening from your heart and inner wisdom instead of your head—helps us get past the limitation of words. Words can sound hollow and intellectual, whereas the experience of what the words are trying to convey can be so full. The gap between the two is bridged by the understanding that comes from insight. Some people get goose bumps when they have the experience of knowing, from deep within, that they are hearing the truth. Others have a knowing that feels like it comes from the heart (or intuition, or spiritual source) even when it may not make sense to the intellect. Just about everyone has had the experience of having an insight that seems to come from nowhere—especially when they couldn't figure something out by thinking about it.

The principles, soon to be explained, help us remember how to bypass the limits of our programmed thought system so we can experience insight. I say "remember" because we were born with that capability and used it as children to enjoy life, to learn, and to experience many beautiful things. Insight is a recognition of a principle or truth which eludes us when we are stuck in the rigid patterns of our thought system.

Remember when you were trying to learn math principles? At first it did not matter how many times you added 2 + 2; it didn't really make sense. Then, suddenly, you caught on and could add any combination of numbers. It made sense that 5 + 7 was the same as 7 + 5. This is one example of experiencing insight to understand a principle. Learning to ride a bicycle or walk a balance beam in gymnastics are other examples. No matter how many times we heard an explanation of the concept of balance, it was beyond our comprehension until we experienced it for ourselves.

We kept plugging away at math and practicing balance, even when the principles made no sense to us. We had to trust that we would eventually learn. Some of us may have practiced out of love for the teacher rather than from faith in future results. Others may have developed a belief that they could not learn and may still have "blocks" about math or balance.

The principles of math and balance do not provide answers. They simply show us how to find answers or how to discover mistakes and make corrections. The principles explained in this book show us how to find answers and make corrections in our lives.

As you read, notice how difficult it can be to hear and understand the principles when you listen only with your intellect. You will know you are in touch with your inner wisdom and inspiration when you read something and have that "aha" feeling—or, upon reading something you disagree with, instead of having negative feelings you are led to a higher understanding that makes more sense to you than the words in this book.

At times you may say with irritation, "But I have heard that before" or "I already know that." When you have "really" heard it at an insight level, you do not get irritated at hearing it again—you feel reaffirmed.

We often hear principles intellectually with just enough understanding to give lip service. When we *understand,* we give heart service. Lip service often includes "shoulds" and "shouldn'ts," or ego gratification. Heart service comes from inner joy, gratitude, and an unconditional desire to be of service to others.

Reading this book could be like putting together a puzzle. Sometimes one piece makes no sense until it fits with another. Perhaps something you read in the middle or at the end will give you the insight to make the beginning more understandable.

This book is short so that it will be easy to read many times. If you get even a glimmer of understanding the first time, you will get more each time you read. Your reading experience will be different as your understanding deepens. When your understanding is deep enough, it will automatically override your limited, programmed thought system and you will access your inherent good feelings and inner wisdom. Several people have told me they keep this book on their bedside table and reread parts at random. They say, "I always seem to choose just the section I need to help me through whatever I am struggling with at the time."

Most of your questions will be answered as you keep reading. The answers will come not from what you read, but from the insight you experience from your own inner wisdom. The purpose of this book is to help you regain greater access to these sources within yourself.

Understanding is the key to natural happiness and peace of mind.

Insight from within is the key to understanding.

Listening softly for a feeling is the key to insight.

This is the cycle. It doesn't matter where you start; each aspect leads in the same direction for positive results in your life and relationships. You are reading this book because you hope to eliminate stress and find serenity, joy, happiness, and peace of mind. Like math and balance, before understanding, principles can seem complicated. After understanding, they seem beautifully simple. When you hear the principles in your heart, you will understand; and you will experience beautiful results in your life.

Keep listening softly.

3

The Principle of Thinking As a Function

You think! This is the best-kept secret of all. *Understanding* that you think is the key to understanding everything else in life.

You may be saying, "That's not a secret. Everyone knows he or she thinks." Actually, very few people remember that thinking is a function or an ability. Instead, they believe that what they think is reality. Most act as though they are passive receivers—or victims—of their thoughts, rather than creators.

In the movie *2001*, scientists create a very sophisticated computer for their space mission. This computer has so many human qualities that it is named Hal. Hal is an amazing servant until, through its human qualities, it develops an ego. Hal stops being a servant and takes over the spaceship.

Truth can be stranger than fiction. Humans have an amazing brain, which can act as an amazing tool. However, through conditioning, we all create a programmed thought system and an ego. The trouble begins when we forget it is our creation and allow it to become our master. The plot thickens when we don't even know we have become servants of a heartless master. We become allies or victims of the misery caused by our programmed thought system by believing in it. We believe in it only when we don't understand that thinking is a function, not a reality.

In her book, *A Return to Love,* Marianne Williamson confirms what happens when we forget that we created our own thought system and ego:

> Thought separated from love is a profound miscreation. It's our own power turned against ourselves. . . . The ego has a pseudo-life of its own, and like all life forms, fights hard for it's survival. . . . The ego is like a virus in the computer that attacks the core system.[1]

Thinking is an ability we use to create our reality. What we think determines what we see—even though we often make the mistake of believing, in an upside-down way, that what we see determines what we think. There is a popular saying, "I'll believe it when I see it." But the truth is reflected in the title of a book by Wayne Dyer, *You'll See It When You Believe It.*[2]

[1]Marriane Williamson, *A Return to Love* (New York: Harper Paperbacks, 1992), p. 35.
[2]Wayne Dyer, *You'll See It When You Believe It* (New York: William Morrow, 1989).

We can think anything we choose to think, and our emotions and actions are then a direct result of what we choose to think. Any form of insecurity, stress, or anxiety results from creating thoughts that produce those kinds of emotions, and then believing that those thoughts are reality rather than products of thinking.[3] For example, try feeling insecure without thinking that you are insecure. It is impossible. As soon as we take the content of our thoughts seriously, we have forgotten that we think.

Joe feels inadequate. He believes his inadequacy is real, and does not recognize it as just a thought. His inadequacy exists because he believes it is real; he bases his behavior on that thought and acts inadequate. (This is why it is not helpful simply to tell people they are adequate. Your belief does not change them. They will feel adequate only when they change their thoughts—or when they access their inner wisdom as discussed below.)

Melissa believes she is depressed because life is overwhelming. But life itself is not overwhelming; only *what she thinks about life* makes it seem overwhelming. This statement can bring up all kinds of debate: "What about disasters, death, war, etc.?" The point I am making is illustrated by two people who had experienced an earthquake. One was living in fear and trying to figure out how to move out of earthquake country. The other said, "This helped me realize what is important in life. I don't need all the

---

[3]Actually there are two levels of feelings: those that come from our thoughts and those that come from our heart or spiritual source. This is discussed further in chapter 4.

17

things I lost in the earthquake. This event was a wake-up call for me to enjoy the more important things in my life, like my family." Some might say, "But what if she lost her family?" The point is illustrated again by two people who lost loved ones. One person went into depression and could not imagine living without her loved one. Another person said, "What a gift it was to have this person in my life for the time I had. I miss him terribly—and I will go on enjoying the many gifts life has to offer."

Many people argue that attitudes are not a product of thinking, but of circumstances. If attitudes were a product of circumstances, however, it would be impossible to find people who still celebrate life even with terminal cancer or crippling afflictions. But there are many happy people who are experiencing all kinds of circumstances in life.

We are often touched and inspired by stories of people who swim without arms, ski without legs, "run" races in wheelchairs, start again after "failures," or celebrate life no matter what the circumstances. Conversely, we could be moved to compassion for people who quit celebrating life because they don't realize that through their thoughts they are making themselves more miserable than their circumstances warrant. It is never the events in our life that create our reality—it is our thoughts about the events.

Some people go through life with the attitude that life is a celebration—something to enjoy fully. Others have the attitude that life is a chore—something to be endured. There is a popular poster expressing this attitude: "Life is hard, and then you die."

Which is it? A celebration or a chore? The answer depends entirely upon what you think.

EXPERIENCING YOUR LIFE THROUGH YOUR THOUGHT SYSTEM OR HEART

Each person has a thought system for storing the memories, perceptions, judgments, and beliefs that act as filters, creating his or her unique, separate reality. (The principle of separate realities is discussed in chapter 5.) Years of accepting beliefs—yours and others'—creates the kind of conditioning that makes illusions seem like reality.[4]

Each individual also has a spiritual source through which he or she can experience wisdom, inspiration, and all the good feelings that are inherent in every human being. There are many names for this spiritual source. Some people call it inner wisdom. Others call it universal wisdom, Spirit, the higher self, the heart, or God. I will use the terms *heart* or *spiritual source* interchangeably or together.

Through our heart or spiritual source, we experience life in a way that is quite different from our mental perceptions. Through our heart, we see life freshly, moment to moment, with fascination, joy, and love. But when we take thoughts from our thought system

---

[4]This is not a condemnation of the thought system. It is a normal phenomenon created and experienced by all of us based on the interpretations and decisions we made as young children when we didn't have the capacity to do anything else. The purpose of this book is simply to help people *understand* the prisons of the mind they have created so they can be free.

seriously, we block our spiritual source and lose access to our inner wisdom and inspiration.

CONDITIONING

We start at an early age to create a thought system, which is made up of our own perceptions and interpretations, as well as those we accept from others. We are very trusting when we are young, usually believing what anyone tells us. Unfortunately, much of what we are told consists of beliefs passed along from generation to generation. This is not done maliciously; our family and friends would not pass on troublesome beliefs if they knew what they were doing. Not knowing any better, they themselves accepted beliefs passed on to them when they were young. Not all beliefs that are passed on are harmful. Many come from the heart or spiritual source and are inherent in the beliefs of every culture: love, gratitude, forgiveness. These beliefs would be lived purely if they weren't contaminated by rigid beliefs and judgments from the thought system. It is the thought system that changes "the spirit of the law" to the "letter of the law."

Most of these beliefs passed on from generation to generation are full of "shoulds" and "shouldn'ts" that contain judgments of worth or worthlessness. We are told how we should be in order to be liked and to be successful. We are also told how others should be and how life should be. We, others, and life hardly ever fit these beliefs, so we live with failure, pseudo-success, anxiety, stress, or disappointment in ourselves, life, and others.

Our thought system also contains such helpful information and skills as reading, writing, arithmetic, names, phone numbers, and the like, which make life easier and more enjoyable. This information is factual and does not create emotions; we use it for our benefit rather than against ourselves.

It is the illusionary thoughts, which create negative emotions, that get us into trouble when we believe they are reality. The beliefs and interpretations we accept or create can seem so real that we live and die for them, even when they make no sense. These beliefs and prejudices are the source of hatred, war, lack of forgiveness, and all insecurities.

Illusionary thinking is often easier to see in other people than it is to see in ourselves. I remember thinking schizophrenics were really crazy when they thought they saw little green bugs crawling up the wall, or when they believed they were Napoleon. It was obvious to me that those were crazy thoughts, whereas all my thoughts, naturally, were serious and real—even the ones that made me miserable.

One psychologist shared that, before she had deeper understanding of these principles, she had a client in therapy who believed a garbage truck was going to eat her. The psychologist spontaneously laughed and said, "That is a silly thought." She had spoken from her common sense and wisdom, but felt a little embarrassed because she had been taught that it is inappropriate to laugh at something a client is taking seriously. Fortunately, the client heard the truth of those words at an even deeper level than they had been spoken, and she began to improve significantly. Several months later the psychologist asked what had made the difference in her recovery. The client replied, "It was the day you told me my thoughts couldn't hurt me."

We all have silly thoughts we take seriously. Yet when we know they are just thoughts, they lose their power to hurt us.

We have power over our programmed thought system when we *understand* it and dismiss it, not when we try to control it. Dismissing our programmed thought system does not mean positive thinking. It does not mean denial. It does not mean repression. It means understanding that thinking is a function, a tool—not a reality. When we understand this, the thought system is automatically dismissed because we see the illusions of our beliefs. Through *understanding* we are automatically transformed through our inherent good feelings, our heart, our spiritual source.

One of my clients quit having panic attacks after hearing the above story about the garbage truck. She said, "The last time a panic attack started, I knew it was just my thoughts. I laughed and felt fine."

I know it is not this simple for everyone. It wasn't for me. Some people understand sooner than others. As I have said before, it seems so difficult until *understanding* makes it so simple.

No one wants the misery created by negative thoughts. Yet some people seem to live as if they do, only because they do not understand the difference between thinking as an expression of wisdom from the heart, and thinking as a reflex of fixed beliefs from their programmed thought system.

The next time you feel upset or miserable, notice what you are thinking. Your emotions are created by your thoughts. Taking your negative thoughts seriously simply means you have forgotten you created them in the first place (often at a subconscious level).[5]

When we realize that thinking is a function or an ability rather than a reality, we can be transformed immediately to our heart or spiritual source where we feel and express our inherent wisdom and good feelings. The first thing our inner wisdom helps us realize is how silly it is to take negative thoughts seriously and base our lives on them.

Many have argued, "Good feelings are not natural to me. It is more natural for me to feel stressed or depressed. I don't try to feel these things; they are just naturally there." But they are not "just naturally" there. There is a negative thought behind every negative feeling.

Can you imagine the problems babies and young children would have if they tried to learn to walk and talk through insecurities produced by a programmed thought system? What would happen if they formed beliefs about falling such as, "Oh dear, I failed again. I am not a very good person. I had better not try again, or I might fall again, and then what would people think?"

---

[5]Please see chapter 8 for more information about subconscious programming. It is often our subconscious programming that produces our present feelings. When this happens, it may appear that our thoughts are caused by our feelings instead of our feelings being caused by our thoughts.

When we rediscover that childlike quality of not thinking through a programmed thought system, our life becomes as much fun as a child's. We lose all forms of insecurity, and each day is full of wonder, adventure, and delight in all there is to experience in life.

If it seems that I am going on and on about this principle, it is because I know this can be the most difficult one to understand. Most people try to figure it out from their programmed thought system. The filters of the thought system created the distortions in the first place, so it is impossible to see things differently through that same perspective. Thus, I am saying the same thing over and over in different ways in hopes that one of the explanations will sneak past your filters and reach your inner wisdom, where all great discoveries and new learning take place.

Looking at life through our programmed thought system is the same as looking at the world through extremely dark glasses labeled "judgment," "blame," "expectations," "pride," "ego," "anger," "shoulds," and other forms of insecurity based on thought. These glasses are like blinders and filters that distort our view of life. The distortion becomes our reality and shuts out everything else, including the truth. Are you wondering, "What *is* the truth?"

The truth is what you see when you take off the dark glasses (dismiss negative thoughts) and access the wisdom of your heart. Have you ever noticed how different everything looks when you replace judgment with compassion, complaints with gratitude, hate with love? Whenever we have any negative feelings, we can recognize that we are wearing one of our pairs of dark glasses. As soon as we dismiss our thoughts, we see from the perspective of our inner wisdom, and our reality changes.

Sometimes you may be aware that you are looking at the world through those dark glasses, but you can't seem to drop them because they feel stuck on with super-glue. It may seem as if you are stuck in your thought system. Knowing what is happening, even when we can't seem to get out of it, shortens the "stuckness" tremendously. It is only thinking about our stuckness, and taking it seriously, perhaps even obsessing about it, that allows it to hang on and get worse. It helps simply to realize what is happening and wait for it to pass rather than to worry about it. It might help to go for a walk, read a good book, meditate, or take a nap. This can be difficult to do if you take your thoughts with you. It is calming when you know you are waiting for the thoughts to pass.[6]

NOT A MATTER OF RIGHT OR WRONG

Understanding the principle of thought as a function does not imply there is a right or wrong way to think. Understanding the principle simply teaches us the many possibilities that come from thinking.

People who believe their thoughts are reality have forgotten the basic fact that they think, and that they

---

[6]Please see chapter 6 for more information on moods, and the importance of getting quiet while waiting for them to pass.

can think anything they want. They have forgotten (or perhaps never understood) that when they change their thoughts, their reality changes.

Sometimes it is very simple. If you don't like what you are thinking about, stop thinking about it.

"But," you may argue, "how can I possibly stop thinking about what I'm thinking? I tried that, and it didn't work."

You keep thinking certain thoughts only when you believe they are reality and take them seriously. When you stop taking them seriously, it takes effort to keep thinking about them. *Understanding* the true nature of thinking makes it difficult to take any of your negative thoughts seriously.

When first learning about the principle of thinking as a function, many people find themselves in variations of the following states of thought.

STATES OF THOUGHT

1. Being caught up in thoughts and taking them seriously.
2. Being caught up in thoughts, but not taking them quite as seriously because of an understanding that they are just thoughts.
3. Being at rest. Dismissing thoughts and getting quiet to wait for inspiration and insight from inner wisdom.
4. Inspiration—when we are experiencing life from our heart or spiritual source.

We are usually in several variations of these states of thought throughout the day. Understanding the principles simply lets us know what is happening, and thus frees us to live more of our life in the third and fourth states listed above.

In Wayne Dyer's *Gifts from Eykis,* Eykis points out, "Thinking is the basis for every single major and minor difficulty you encounter. The problems that arise in politics, religion, education, families, business, the military, society, medicine, and every form of human enterprise are due to self-programmed unreal thinking."[7]

When we understand our programmed thought system for the filter that it is, we will be able to bypass it, except for occasional short visits. When we understand what happens when we are there, we won't want to stay for long. Each visit will simply confirm that thinking through our programmed thought system does not produce happiness and peace of mind (unless, of course, we are using it to remember useful facts and skills). Staying too long in states one or two may be letting us know we have some healing to do.

SEEKING HELP

Sometimes our programmed thoughts and beliefs are so deeply embedded that they keep causing us problems—emotionally, physically, and spiritually. Dismissing our programmed thought system may give us temporary relief, but those subconscious beliefs keep returning and affecting our behavior and our health.

[7]Wayne Dyer, *Gifts from Eykis* (New York: Pocket Books, 1983), pp. 118–119.

We don't even know what thoughts we need to dismiss. They are beyond our conscious awareness. We are, however, profoundly aware of the misery they cause.

There is a wonderful story about a little girl who went to camp. During the day and evening, she was enthralled with all the activities, new friends, and story-telling around the bonfire. However, that evening a counselor found her crying in her bed. The counselor tried to comfort her in every way she could think of. Finally she said, "God is always with you." The little girl said, "I know, but I want someone with skin on."

There are times when we all need a friend with skin on. Sometimes we need help from others who can comfort us or, when we are ready, show us another perspective.

We may need help from others to heal programmed thoughts and beliefs. Yes, beliefs can be healed, just as physical wounds can be healed. Positive thinking does not heal beliefs. Denial does not heal, and neither does repression. Beliefs are healed when the lie is exposed and understanding takes place. In her book, *Heal the Cause,* Valerie Seeman Moreton writes, "When faulty programming is exposed and released, great relief is experienced. A light, open feeling of gratitude comes in and fills the empty space left by the old lie."[8]

When beliefs are healed, people don't have to *try* to give up the misconception that they are inadequate,

---

[8]Valerie Seeman Moreton, N.D., *Heal the Cause* (San Diego: Kalos Publishing, 1996), p. 64.

unloved, or can't forgive. They couldn't hang on to those beliefs if they tried. Healing takes us immediately to our heart where we feel love and compassion for self and others. We can't judge, because we see the innocence of the people we believed had intentionally hurt us.

Some find help that heals their beliefs by reading a book or talking with a friend. Others gain insights and inspiration in a church or a personal growth workshop. Others find help from therapy. No matter where you seek help, the criterion to look for is information or a process that helps you get beyond your programmed thought system and into your heart or spiritual source.

A wonderful part of healing is that we see the perfection of all things. Moreton puts it this way:

> Sometimes seeing the benefit of what has happened defuses deeply held emotions even further. Seeing the benefit of the situation creates a deeper understanding of how the universe is always working to support our highest good. . . . Acknowledging that benefit makes us more conscious of what is real and why forgiveness is always expedient. You can actually be happy about an uncomfortable experience when you see that a benefit has come from it. You can actually be grateful for it. Love and gratitude release healing energy during a Process.[9]

Looking for the gift or life lesson in every situation is discussed more thoroughly in chapter 4.

[9]Moreton, pp. 269–270.

THINKING IS NOT "THE BAD GUY"

At this point, or sooner, many people get the notion that thinking is "the bad guy," and we should not think. Not at all. Thinking is a beautiful gift through which we experience the beauty of life. The key is understanding *where thoughts originate.* When they originate in our programmed thought system we usually do not experience peace of mind and satisfaction. We experience serenity when thinking is the means we use to experience or express our inner wisdom, inspiration, and inherent good feelings that originate in our heart or from our spiritual source.

We are almost always thinking. *Understanding* helps us dismiss negative thoughts which come from our programmed thought system and to enjoy a nice life from our heart or spiritual source.

4

The Principle of Feelings As a Compass

Our feelings are like a compass, letting us know where we are on our treasure map. Unconditional positive feelings act as a compass to let us know we are experiencing life from our heart or spiritual source. When we feel bad emotionally, we are off course into our programmed thought system. Remember: It is impossible to have negative feelings without thoughts from our thought system. Thus, negative feelings act as a compass that lets us know that.

Just as Eskimos have many words to describe snow, we need many words to describe feelings. The feelings that come from our heart are very different from those that come from our programmed thought system. Heart feelings are unconditional, and they include a sense of peace, gratitude, love, and wisdom.

It is possible to have positive feelings from the thought system, but they are conditional and temporary. For example, we may feel good if we win the lottery, until we discover that money doesn't buy happiness. We may feel good when we find our "true love," until we discover that many of those feelings were based on expectations and illusions from our thought system. True love is unconditional and everlasting.

While first learning about the principles, I believed *understanding* meant I would never have negative feelings again, and I became very disappointed in myself whenever I took my thoughts seriously. By doing this, I had flipped out of my heart and into my head, where I used the information against myself. My feelings compass let me know this, and that it was time to stop thinking about it and get quiet.

Before long, understanding led me back to my inner wisdom that let me know it did not matter that my negative thoughts kept creeping in. (They were not actually "creeping" in. We become so proficient at instantaneously pulling up "files" from our programmed thought system that we forget they are still our moment-to-moment creations. It then seems that thoughts creep into our mind beyond our control, which is impossible.) After this realization, I experienced just "watching" those thoughts without judging them. I even felt a tolerant affection for my negative thoughts. I started seeing them as interesting or "humorous." When I understood they were just thoughts, they could not hurt me. Most of the time, I could laugh and dismiss them. I have since learned that when it seems I can't dismiss them, they could be blessings in disguise—waiting for me to use them as opportunities for greater learning and healing.

All of us have subconscious beliefs based on decisions we made as children formed from our perceptions at the time. Certain events may trigger emotional reactions from the past that are beyond our present awareness. Until we heal these *perception prisons,* thoughts and emotions do seem to "creep" in.

We all get off course into our thought system on a daily basis—some of us more often than others. Understanding helps us to not take getting off course seriously, to not judge ourselves, and to be open for the inspiration or healing that leads us back on course.

A word of caution: Many people claim they are just following their feelings compass when they do negative things, like "getting out" their anger, or telling another person that their judgments about them are "the truth." This is a misuse of the feelings compass discussed in this chapter.

An understanding of this principle does not mean we will never feel sad, hurt, or angry; it means that when we use these feelings as a compass, we will look to see where they are coming from—the thought system or the heart. Sometimes we may experience feelings from our inner wisdom that *seem* similar to those from the thought system. While similar, they are totally different. As an example, I will paraphrase something I heard Wayne Dyer say in one of his lectures: "It angers and saddens me to see hunger in the world, but I know everything is in Divine Order. It is perfect that there is hunger in the world, and it is perfect that I want to do something about it." Instead of ranting and raving about the injustice of hunger, Wayne contributes regularly to the World Hunger Fund and does everything he can to raise the world consciousness to a level where hunger could not take place.

Unconditional good feelings and actions flow naturally from the heart. The feeling comes first and is then experienced through the function of thinking. Negative feelings are experienced after we create negative thoughts from our thought system. In other words, if the feeling comes first, it is from the heart; if the feeling comes second, it is from your thought system.[1] For example, you see a newborn baby and your heart is filled with wonder. The feeling of wonder comes first and then is processed through your function of thinking. On the other hand, you may have fearful thoughts about negative conditions in the world. You see a newborn baby and feel sad because of what this poor child will have to live through. The thoughts come first and affect your feelings.

Soon after learning this I had an experience that illustrates how thought can affect feeling. During a one-week seminar in which I was learning about the principles, I called home to see how my children were doing. I was informed that my thirteen-year-old son had been suspended from school.

---

[1]Again, I wish we had more words to describe feelings. A feeling that is triggered from the subconscious may seem to come first, but it is not an "in the moment" feeling. It is a feeling based on subconscious thoughts from the past.

This is how he told the story: "I found some cigarettes in my locker. I don't know how they got there. I was just putting them in my pocket to take them to the principal when a teacher came by and took me to the principal."

It felt as though my thoughts went crazy for a few minutes (but actually I created crazy thoughts): "He is lying to us. I'm a failure as a mother. If he's smoking cigarettes, he's probably also using alcohol and drugs. He is going to ruin his life. What will people think?" I was very upset, so my feelings compass let me know loud and clear that I was caught up in my thought system and was not seeing clearly. I dismissed my feelings compass instead of my thoughts for a minute and used more thoughts to bury my inner wisdom: "Yes, but this is different. These are really terrible circumstances over which I have no control. How could I possibly see them differently? I am going to have to scold him severely, ground him for at least a month, take away all his privileges, and let him know he is ruining his life." Fortunately, I had too much faith in the principles to take those thoughts seriously, and inspiration quickly surfaced. I then saw the circumstances in a completely different way and felt understanding and compassion for my son's view of the situation. He had just entered junior high school, where the pressure is enormous to follow the crowd rather than to follow common sense.

When I got home, I listened to my inspiration and knew what to do. I sat down with my son, put my arm around him, and said, "I'll bet it's tough trying to figure out how to say no to your friends so you won't be called a nerd or a party pooper." He had been expecting my usual craziness and hardly knew how to respond to my sanity.

He said tentatively, "Yeah."

I went on, "And I'll bet the only reason you would ever lie to us is because you love us so much you don't want to disappoint us." Tears filled his eyes, and he gave me a big hug. With tears in my own eyes, I reassured him, "If you think you could ever disappoint us enough to diminish our love, then we are not doing a good enough job of letting you know how much we love you, unconditionally."

We can only guess what the results would have been had I followed my crazy thoughts to interact with my son. My guess is that my craziness would have inspired increased rebelliousness instead of increased closeness. No matter what the results, my inner wisdom lets me know that he has a right to live his own life and learn his own lessons. I know he will have a much better chance to experience his inner wisdom if he feels unconditional love from me instead of my ego's need to judge him.

I am continually grateful for the principle of using my feelings as a compass to let me know when I am "off track." Whenever I feel upset, angry, judgmental, disappointed, or any other negative emotion, I know my feelings are being created by thoughts I am taking seriously. As soon as I recognize that and dismiss the thoughts, I am filled with my inherent good feelings.

Dismissing negative thoughts is not the same as sticking your head in the sand. It is more like taking off blinders and filters so you can see the situation with perspective. Sometimes the problem disappears along with the negative thoughts. Other times the problem may still be there, but you are able to view it differently. You will see solutions rather than problems, because from your inner wisdom, solutions are clear.

FEELINGS COMPASS CHART

The following chart has helped many people use their feelings compass to increase their *understanding.* It is a graphic representation of the feelings and conditions we experience from our heart, and those we experience when thinking from our programmed thought system.

Heart or Spiritual Source	*Programmed Thought System*
High level of consciousness	*Low level of consciousness*
Security	Insecurity
Love	Expectations
Serenity and happiness	Stress and coping
Compassion	Judgments
Contentment	Wanting more, better, different
Wisdom	Rules (shoulds and shouldn'ts)

Forgiveness	Blame, anger, self-righteousness
Gratitude	Blindness to miracles
Inspiration	Beliefs
Peace of mind	Depression and/or anxiety
The beauty of now	Past- or future-oriented
Natural positive feelings	Positive thinking

Try adding other words to the columns. A word such as *responsibility* feels like duty or compulsiveness when added to the thought-system column. Responsibility feels natural and easy when added to the heart column. Notice how different *sex* feels in either column, or *charity, strength, giving, discipline, teaching, control, desire,* or any other concept you can think of.

Even so-called positive attributes can come from the thought system instead of the heart. *Admiration* is an example. Put that word in each column and see how the meaning changes. Is your admiration based on your perception that a person has met your expectations, done the "right thing," or done a good job of proving his ego? Or is admiration based on unconditional love and gratitude? Can you admire a person as you would a flower or a sunset?

Also notice what happens when you take some of the words from the heart column and add them to the thought-system column. Love and forgiveness, for example, do not have the same feeling when shifted. How many of us have experienced the contamination of love when we add expectations and judgments? How many of us have felt self-righteous for forgiving?

Again, I want to clarify that I'm not saying any of this is wrong. *Understanding* the principles gives us a road map to where we are; it doesn't tell us where we *should* be. We have already discussed that there are gifts to be found and lessons to be learned from our experiences through our thought system. Of course, as soon as we see this, we have returned to our heart or spiritual source.

We all go in and out of these states of mind every day, depending on what thoughts we are thinking. Remembering that thinking is an ability makes it natural to quit taking our thoughts seriously and leave room for heart messages. These messages will immediately change our state of mind and our feelings. Mental illness or mental health is simply a moment-to-moment state of mind. Mental illness and unhappiness are states that occur when we forget that thinking is a function.

POSITIVE THINKING

Did you wonder why positive thinking was in the column on the right? The feelings and wisdom we experience from our heart or spiritual source are different from what we experience through positive thinking. Positive thinkers forget they have the ability to think, and try to change thoughts instead of dismissing them and allowing wisdom to surface naturally. They assume that thoughts "happen" to them, and that, through positive thinking, they can control which thoughts happen or can change the ones that have already happened. They are dealing with thinking as a reality rather than as a function.

When we are enjoying a beautiful sunset or feeling love, wouldn't it be ridiculous to stop and say, "I'd better start thinking positively about this"? Even to have the *thought* of positive thinking means we are having negative thoughts, which we think we "should" change. No "shoulds" are involved when we are in our hearts—just natural, positive feelings and obvious things to do to experience positive results in our lives and relationships. The battleground is eliminated. If we are experiencing a battle in our minds, we are operating from our thought system, not from our heart.

Positive thinking is also conditional: "I will be happy if I have positive thoughts," or, "I'm a success when I think positively, and a failure when I don't." It is true that we will be happy if we have positive thoughts, but when positive thoughts come from our hearts, they are natural and effortless. Have you ever wanted to think positively, but felt like a failure because you couldn't? Perhaps what you are learning now will help you understand why it seems to work sometimes and not others.

Annie experienced a failure of positive thinking after a fight with her brother. She went into her room and tried to forget about it by thinking of enjoyable things. First she thought about baseball, but that didn't work because she just wanted to hit her brother with a bat. Then she tried thinking about soccer, but felt like kicking her brother instead of the ball.

When Annie realized that no kind of thinking helped, she stopped thinking and started looking out the window. She quietly watched the birds and enjoyed looking at the trees and flowers, and soon, instead of thinking positively or negatively about the past, she became engrossed in the present. Before long, Annie felt good again. She apologized to her brother, and spent the rest of the afternoon playing with him.

Positive thinking comes from our programmed thought system and takes effort. It is not necessary when we use our thinking ability for the natural expression of beautiful feelings, which come through our heart in all the positive forms, such as inspiration, gratitude, and unconditional love.

When you are experiencing any stress or unhappiness in your life, it may help to take a look at the Feelings Compass Chart. Use your feelings compass. Allow your inner wisdom to let you know what thoughts or beliefs from the column on the right are causing your misery. As soon as you "see" it, that *understanding* may allow you to drop those thoughts and access your heart.

It is amazing how different we feel when we see the world from our hearts or spiritual source. Love, joy, compassion, and wisdom flow.

41

5

The Principle of Separate Realities

Another well-kept secret is the fact that everyone lives in a separate reality. This simply means that we all interpret things differently and each view the world from our own private logic. A popular example often used to explain the principle of separate realities is that everyone who sees an accident describes it differently. The reason becomes obvious when we understand that everyone sees through the filters of his or her own unique, programmed thought system.

We have separate realities because everyone has personal memories, interpretations, and beliefs that act like filters through which present events are seen. When we view the world through these filters, it is impossible to see what *is* with fresh perspective.

Again, you may object, "Everyone knows that." It is true that most of us have heard this principle, but we forget to apply it in our lives. Hearing about separate realities and *understanding* the principle at a deep level are not the same. When we really understand the fact of separate realities, we will stop spending so much time and energy trying to change the reality of others. Remember, there is a difference between understanding from an intellectual level (from our heads) and understanding from insight (from our hearts).

Without *understanding*, we are unaware of our filters, and we therefore think our interpretations are real. We become convinced that if we try hard enough we can persuade others that our reality is the right one. This *never works*—so marriages may break up in hostility, parents and children experience "generation gaps," and nations go to war. The reverse can also apply. Some people think their reality is wrong, or is not as good as other people's, and so they may spend a lot of time feeling inadequate, insecure, and depressed.

When we don't understand separate realities, we have thoughts such as, "How could they possibly be like that or do that? They would be happier if they did it my way, liked my kind of music (especially at the volume I prefer), ate the foods I like, and loaded the dishwasher the way I do." These thoughts and judgments can create a great deal of misery in the form of anger or other stressful emotions.

I had an opportunity to learn this *again* when I became very upset with one of my children. The details aren't as important as the lesson. I knew I was deeply stuck in my thought system, and couldn't seem to drop it. I kept wondering, "How could he do that?" I couldn't understand how he could justify his behavior.

Finally, I sat down to meditate and ask for messages from my heart, which came almost immediately. The first was, *You wonder how he could have done such a thing. How many times in your life have you done things that would invite the same question from others? It is his life to live.*

I don't mean that I heard a voice, exactly. This is simply an example of the kind of wisdom that is expressed in thoughts that come from our heart or spiritual source instead of our programmed thought system. The message seemed so obvious once I "heard" it, but I couldn't hear it while stuck in the perception prison of my thought system.

This is an example of the mirror insight process (described in chapter 7). Often, whatever we find annoying in someone else is really a reflection of an area where we need some work ourselves. We often don't want to see this, especially when we think that what the other person does is so much worse than what we do. With *understanding* we can see the humor in this. If what we do is less serious, how much better our time could be spent correcting our own foibles than judging others. As I have said before, a message from our heart often seems humorous when we finally *see* it.

Other messages from my inner wisdom followed: *Look at the trouble you create for yourself when you think others should live up to your expectations or do "what is right" and "for their own good" according to you.*

I had to laugh at my self-righteousness when I *saw* it. I had believed that my son's actions had made me miserable; instead, I remembered that *my thoughts about what he did* made me miserable. I felt gratitude for the lesson and compassion for my son.

When we truly *understand* the principle of separate realities, we see differences with a more compassionate interest. We may prefer not to spend time with some people whose reality creates negative energy. This choice, however, will be made with compassion for them and respect for ourselves, rather than with negative judgments and self-righteousness.

We usually respect separate realities when visiting another country; we certainly wouldn't be welcome if we told people of other countries that they should speak our language and change their customs. Traveling is enjoyable when we learn about different cultures and traditions, and respect differences. Wouldn't it be wonderful if we approached personal relationships with the same wonder and respect?

Phil and Lisa experienced separate realities soon after they were married. Phil was an "early bird"; he loved getting up at dawn full of energy and ready to enjoy the day. Every morning he bounded out of bed and sang loudly in the shower, hoping Lisa would wake up.

Noticing her still in bed with the covers pulled over her head, he would noisily bounce on the bed as he put on his shoes and socks, thinking, "If she really loved me, she would get up and enjoy this time with me."

Lisa, totally annoyed at what she saw as his "inconsiderateness," would be thinking, "If he really loved me, he would know I hate getting up early and would be quiet and let me sleep."

They often discussed their differences, but neither really "heard" the other because each was more interested in changing, than in understanding, the other. They both felt like they were talking to a wall as they tried to make their points. What they did not realize is that they were talking to two walls—the wall of their own reality as well as the wall of the other's reality.

Christmases were a disaster. When Lisa was growing up, everyone in her family had received one very nice, expensive present for Christmas. In Phil's family everyone had enjoyed the fun of opening several inexpensive presents. So Lisa would buy Phil one nice, expensive present, and Phil would buy Lisa several inexpensive presents. Every Christmas they felt disappointed and misunderstood, each thinking the other was too dense to know how to really enjoy Christmas.

We may be amused at Phil and Lisa for not seeing how simply they could solve their problems by respecting their separate realities instead of by trying to change each other. Nonetheless, when dealing with our own precious beliefs, we are often just as blind.

Have you noticed how important it seems to tell others, especially those we love, when we think they are wrong? Then we wonder why they don't appreciate it.

Bill used to dread visiting his father because they both always ended up with bad feelings. Bill said, "We used to spend all our time together arguing about who was right and who was wrong. I was certainly never going to admit I was wrong, because it seemed very clear to me that I wasn't. Dad would not admit he was wrong, even though I made every effort to let him know how old-fashioned his ideas were. *Understanding* separate realities was a godsend for me. Dad and I no longer argue over our differences. I respect how he sees things and know I would see them the same way if I were in his shoes. Now we just share the love and gratitude we have and enjoy each other's company."

Nor is it helpful to judge your own reality. One day when I was judging myself for not having a deeper understanding of the principles, I suddenly realized that any form of judgment would only block my *understanding*. When I stopped judging my present reality, I could see that to say I should be farther along than I am, or that someone else should have a different reality than he or she does, makes as much sense as saying a rosebud should be a rose in full bloom.

Every human being is in the process of evolving, learning, and growing (or refusing to change). Getting in the way with our judgments only creates negativity and impedes progress. Can you imagine how much more helpful we would be to ourselves and others if we were loving and compassionate instead of judgmental?

A master gardener does not fret because her roses are not growing into petunias, but simply nurtures all of the flowers with water, weeding, and fertilizer so they can reach their full potential as roses, petunias, or whatever they are. We can likewise simply enjoy and nurture who we and others are.

"Shoulds" are not necessary when we have access to our inherent good feelings. Nurturing ourselves and others comes naturally from the heart. Our inner wisdom lets us know that the key is to love and nurture, not to judge.

Some people have put this information into their thought system and misused it. I have heard people say in a disparaging tone of voice, "Well, that is just your separate reality, and I have a right to mine." This was not said from love, compassion, and respect. *Understanding* can never be used against others—or ourselves.

Our world expands greatly when we understand and appreciate separate realities. It is possible to enjoy differences (or at least understand them) instead of fighting over them. When we quit seeing separate realities as right or wrong, we see ourselves and others without judgment, and we are free from the negative feelings that cloud our vision when we are judgmental. People who insist that they must be judgmental to keep the world from "going to hell" put themselves in a state of mental hell, which does not help the world. Love energy helps the world. If you cannot find it in your heart to love a negative person, at least love yourself enough to stay out of his or her way, without judgment.

If your programmed thought system is resisting, you are probably dredging up the worst possible examples you can imagine, such as murder, rape, and burglary—or a spouse who did some terrible thing. Self-righteousness, hatred, or any form of negative judgment only keeps you separated from your heart and inner wisdom that could lead you to positive action. You then become like the thing or person you judge or hate, spreading more negativity in the world. When you live from your heart, you will know what to do about these issues to get the best possible results. You will act from love and wisdom.

You may argue, "But some things really are wrong!" With understanding we see that this need not be an issue, because everyone does the best he can with what he knows. When we see the innocence in all behavior and feel compassion or interest, instead of judgment, we are much happier. We can't help anyone else when we are unhappy. And when we have understanding, it is natural to "forgive them, for they know not what they do." However, *we* will know what to do. It is natural to follow the Serenity Prayer when we wish to experience life from our spiritual source:

> *God, grant me the serenity to accept the things I cannot change, the courage to change the things I can, and the wisdom to know the difference.*

All relationships can be enhanced through an *understanding* of the principle of separate realities. It is often said that many people would rather be *right* than be loved. In the thought system, this seems to be the case.

I recently had the opportunity to recognize that I was choosing to be "right" instead of choosing love. My husband and I were getting ready to come home from a large convention. He wanted to get in line for the hotel shuttle to the airport two hours early. I wanted to get in line one hour early. We were both getting annoyed at what we perceived to be obtuse behavior in the other. Each of us thought the reality of the other was ridiculous.

My feelings compass gave me a wake-up call and I consciously chose to go into my heart. From that space I said to Barry, "I wonder what would happen if we looked at this differently and had compassion for what it would cost either of us to follow the lead of the other. The price I would have to pay to go early is the discomfort of spending more time at the airport. The price you would have to pay is worry and anxiety about being late."

It was obvious to me that it would be easier for me to change than for him—because I had moved into my heart. From my heart, I saw his separate reality as endearing instead of wrong. I also saw the benefits of getting to the airport in plenty of time to relax. I saw how I could learn from him when I quit seeing his point of view as ridiculous.

Some people could see this as a technique—but the key was moving out of my head and into my heart where everything looked and felt different. It was contagious. Barry felt loved and responded by moving into his heart. He said, "Well, I guess I do exaggerate." We laughed, left for the airport early, and had a good time being together.

Being loving and loved is much nicer than being "right." In the heart, where separate realities are seen with interest and compassion, loving has top priority.

6

The Principle of Mood Levels, or Levels of Consciousness

Everyone has moods. Some people seem to fluctuate between extremes more than others, but we all experience times when we feel good and times when we feel low. Have you noticed how different your own separate reality is, depending on whether you're feeling high or low? In different moods, it is possible to see the same things differently. For example, recall the last time you were driving along in a good mood and someone needed to cut in front of you, and you cheerfully waved them in, remembering how often you have been in the same situation. Now, think of another time when you were in a low mood and you stepped on the gas, determined not to let them in, mumbling about how stupid and inconsiderate *they* were. When we are in a low mood, everything looks bad. We may feel overwhelmed and have feelings of impending doom. There seems to be no way out.

Higher moods or levels of consciousness simply mean that we can see things with more perspective and with greater *understanding* from our heart or spiritual source. Lower moods or levels of consciousness simply mean that we have lost perspective and understanding because we are living in our programmed thought system.

Reality is greatly distorted with lost perspective. The distortion is heavily sprinkled with ego, expectations, and judgments. At a time of lost perspective, however, our distorted thoughts seem like the only possibility.

Sometimes low moods just happen as part of our physiological functioning. It makes sense to simply wait for them to pass. Usually, however, a belief or thought is the culprit. Often we are unaware of the thoughts that have created our low moods. Trying to figure out the cause usually makes things worse, because we are trying to figure it out from the very thought system that created the low mood. The secret is knowing that moods are not nearly as bad as the thoughts we have about them. The key is to patiently wait for the mood to pass.

I remember when I used to get depressed. Feeling inadequate and insecure about something, I would retreat into depression. Then I would be upset with myself for being depressed, thereby feeling more inadequate and insecure. How depressing! I did not understand the vicious cycle I was creating with my thoughts. Later, I started looking forward to my depressions because I used them as an excuse to lie in bed all day and read. My depressions quit lasting very long when I started enjoying them. I finally saw the obvious and realized I did not have to get depressed in order to take a day to rest and enjoy myself. I could simply follow my inner wisdom, which was letting me know it was time to get quiet.

A quiet mind is the best cure for a low mood. You have a quiet mind naturally when you dismiss thoughts from your programmed thought system. Sometimes the simple realization that "it is only a mood" will be enough to immediately raise your level of consciousness. The moment this happens your thoughts will be dismissed, and you will have access to your heart, from which you can see things from a higher perspective. Your reality will change.

Ellen was upset because a department store had failed to refund her money as promised. She took out her anger on the customer service clerk, who talked back rudely to Ellen. As soon as Ellen realized what was happening, her mood shifted and she saw things differently. She then said to the clerk, "You really have a tough job, don't you?"

The clerk responded immediately, in a better mood, "I sure do." From then on she was very helpful, and the problem was resolved.

It all goes back to thought. In lower levels of consciousness, we react from a thought system full of troublesome beliefs and judgments. In higher levels of consciousness, it is natural to see things with love, joy, gratitude, or simple interest. When action needs to be taken, we know what to do to increase love instead of fear.

It is impossible to see anything with *understanding* when we are in a low mood. It makes no sense to trust our thoughts or feelings when we are in a low level of consciousness because they are being filtered through our programmed thought system rather than coming from wisdom and common sense. Understanding this principle teaches us to get quiet (verbally, physically, and mentally) and wait for the low mood to pass.

Don't underestimate the power of quiet to help you let go of troublesome thoughts and move into your heart. Be gentle with yourself. It may take several days or weeks. Looking for the life lesson or benefit of your situation may help. If you think another person has contributed to your low mood, looking in "the mirror" might help—when you see your reflection with insight, humor, and compassion. Prolonged low moods may be letting you know that you have some out-of-awareness thoughts and beliefs that need healing. When you can't seem to access your own inner wisdom, it is fine to seek the help of someone who has access to theirs. I would not suggest seeking help from anyone who does not understand the importance of leading you out of your programmed thought system and into your inner wisdom.

NOW YOU SEE IT, NOW YOU DON'T

High or low moods (or levels of consciousness) are not a matter for value or moral judgment. Consciousness is a state of awareness, perspective, or insight. Sometimes we see it (*understand*), and sometimes we don't. The moment we *understand* that we are seeing things from a lower level of consciousness, we have jumped to a higher level of consciousness. It takes *understanding* to realize when we are not seeing something with understanding. So, the moment we recognize we have not been *seeing* clearly, we are seeing that much more clearly. However, if in the next moment we judge ourselves because we didn't see clearly initially, we lose our understanding again. Be gentle with yourself.

When we are in a good mood or higher level of consciousness we feel love, compassion, forgiveness, and gratitude. We feel satisfaction and peace of mind. We see things with greater understanding and perspective. We do not have to try to make ourselves feel these things through positive thinking; in a higher level of consciousness, we feel them naturally.

You may ask, "What about all those times when I am not in a good mood or at a higher level of consciousness? How do I get out of my low mood if I don't try to figure it out or use positive thinking?"

Feeling low happens, just as storms happen. We don't try to figure out how to stop a storm, or why it is there, or how to change it. We simply do whatever is necessary to minimize damage, make ourselves as comfortable as possible, and wait for the storm to pass.

A sailor knows the importance of dropping the sails when coming into a storm. With understanding, we know the importance of dropping negative thoughts when we are in a low mood or have any negative feelings.

Low moods can change immediately with recognition, or, like the flu, they may hang around even when we know what they are. When we get the flu, we know that the best thing to do is to take care of ourselves until it passes; we are also careful not to spread it around. It is wise to treat your low moods in the same way.

Understanding the principle of mood levels helps us know how effective it is to get quiet and wait for low moods to pass—or to know enough not to spread our bad moods around—or to forgive ourselves and others when we don't have enough understanding to snap out of it or wait for it to pass. There are many levels of understanding.

Some people suppose that there is only one level of understanding, and that once you have it you will never lose it again. This has not been my experience, however, nor the experience of anyone I know. An understanding of math principles doesn't mean we will never make a mistake in addition. However, math principles will help us find the mistake and correct it.

It now seems perfect to me that we get lost in our programmed thought system once in a while. We can also find so many gifts in the experience. Of course, while we are lost, it is impossible to see the gifts. It is not helpful to beat up on ourselves. *It is helpful to know that it is normal, and that we can't see it until we see it.* Using the principles can help us understand what happened and how to find our way back to *understanding,* where we see the gifts and feel gratitude.

GRATITUDE

I have found that one of the quickest ways to change my mood is through gratitude. It is difficult to hang on to silly thoughts while appreciating all there is to be grateful for. Once I was in such a sour mood I couldn't think of anything to be grateful for. Then I looked down at my hands and was struck by the absolute miracle of my ability to move my fingers. Then I looked up and saw the sky. How beautiful! Love, beauty, and miracles are all around us whenever we are willing to notice. When we are stuck in our thought system, we miss so much. We could be walking on a spectacular beach or through a beautiful forest and miss all the beauty if our focus is on troublesome thoughts—just as we miss simple pleasures and the joy of personal relationships.

Sue Pettit had a wonderful insight about moods and thoughts, and was inspired to write a poem entitled "Lily's Loose."[1] Notice the similarity of Lily Tomlin's role as Ernestine at the switchboard from the old TV show, *Laugh-In,* and what happens when we let our thought system take over.

---

[1]"Lily's Loose" and many other wonderful poems, which beautifully and humorously illustrate the principles of Psychology of Mind, are available in a book entitled *Coming Home* by Sue Pettit, published by Sunrise Press, Fair Oaks, California (800-456-7770).

Lily's Loose

Lily is the operator at the switchboard of my
  brain.
And when she starts reacting, my life becomes
  insane.
She's supposed to be employed by me—and
  play a passive role.
But anytime I'm insecure—Lily takes control.

Lily's loose, Lily's loose, Lily's loose today.
Tell everyone around me just to clear out of
  my way.
The things I say won't make much sense—all
  COMMON SENSE is lost.
'Cause when Lily's at the switchboard—my
  wires all get crossed.

Lily is my own creation, thought I needed her
  with me
To organize and then recall all my life's history.
But she started taking liberty with all my
  information.
And whenever she starts plugging in—I get a
  bad sensation.

Lily's loose, Lily's loose, Lily's loose today.
Tell all my friends and relatives to clear out of
  my way.
I don't give hugs and kisses when I'm in this
  frame of mind.
And please don't take me seriously—it'd be a
  waste of time.

She looks out through my eyeballs and sees
   what I do see.
Then hooks up wires to my past—she thinks
   she's helping me!
When I'm in a good mood, I can smile at her
   endeavor.
But when I'm in a bad mood—Lily's boss, and
   is she clever.

Lily's loose, Lily's loose, Lily's loose today.
Tell the world to hurry by and stay out of my
   way.
I'm feeling very scattered—I'm lost in my
   emotion.
Lily's on a rampage, and she's causing a
   commotion.

   I heard a wonderful story from a lady in Connecti-
cut who said she read this poem to her teenage son.
Then, every time she would start lecturing or scolding,
one of them would see what was happening and say,
"Lily's Loose," and both would start laughing.

LAUGHTER

Laughter has the power to transform moods. With *understanding*, it is difficult to take things too seriously.
The seriousness is usually based on thoughts and beliefs from the thought system that incorporate judgments, shoulds, and shouldn'ts. Our control issues can
seem particularly funny when seen with perspective.
   I had an interesting insight about control while
on a ski hill. I was snow-plowing so I would have

more control. It was a lot of work—and not much fun. Then, I looked up the hill and saw the expert skiers. They were not snow-plowing or demonstrating any other kind of "controlling behavior," yet they seemed to have perfect control—and were having lots of fun. I realized that their control came from a mastery of skiing techniques and principles, not from behavior that provided an illusory sense of control.

I applied this insight to relationships between teachers and students, parents and children, and husbands and wives. When we stop our controlling behavior (which comes from fear and insecurity) and apply principles of love, dignity, and respect, control doesn't seem to be an issue. We naturally have control without acting controlling. We don't try to make people change, yet we are often inspired to do things that may invite change. The inspiration we receive often includes humor.

In our parenting workshops, we suggest that parents quit taking many things seriously and adopt an "isn't it cute" attitude around some things that upset them. I was driving myself crazy over the fact that my teenagers kept leaving empty cereal bowls in their rooms. Not only could I never find a cereal bowl when I needed one, but the bowls in their rooms were caked with dried cereal and sour milk. I ranted and raved until I used my feelings compass to realize I was obviously coming from my thought system. As soon as I dismissed my judgments, I really could see it as a cute, teenage phenomenon. Then I was inspired to take action from love and humor. We discussed the "problem" at a family meeting. After laughing about how normal it is for teenagers to do things like this, we came up with a solution. Every other week I would daily collect their cereal bowls as a reminder to myself of how much I love them. Every other week they would bring their cereal bowls to the dishwasher out of love for me. Since I know how easy it is for teenagers to get distracted from things that are a priority to adults, we agreed that it would be fine for me to put a love note on their pillows when they forgot. This worked much better than all the ranting and raving—and was a lot more fun.

Nothing I did from my thought system was effective. Those actions created rebellion, anger, and frustration. None of us felt loved. What I did from my heart created love and harmony—and a solution that was effective.

HELPING OTHERS IN A LOW MOOD

So-called "techniques" feel very different when coming from *understanding* than when coming from the thought system. The technique of *reflective listening* provides a good example. Reflective listening simply means to validate what a person is saying by reflecting the words back. When we do this from our thought system, we often sound like a parrot. When *understanding* takes us to our heart, we reflect feelings, as well as words, out of compassion. We don't take the words of others so seriously because we know they are coming from a low mood, or beliefs from the programmed thought system. People we are listening to do not need "advice" from our thought system. They need compassion from our heart, as in the following example.

Sally was very angry at her sister because of an argument that had taken place two years ago. The sister wanted to come for a visit, but Sally refused to see her. Her husband, Joel, gave her some "spiritual" advice. "Don't you think it is time to let go of your anger and learn to forgive? Don't you know how much this anger is hurting you?"

Sally did not find the "advice" helpful. She felt hurt, and told Joel, "You just don't understand."

Joel shared what had happened with a friend who had an *understanding* of the four principles. She asked Joel, "What do you think would happen if you stopped seeing the details of what she is saying, and instead saw her as a person who is caught up in her thought system and is in a very low mood? Try giving her compassion through reflective listening instead of advice."

That night Joel apologized to Sally for giving her advice, and said, "I can understand how hurt you felt by the argument with your sister."

Sally responded defensively, "It seems like everytime I try to get close to her, she says something mean to me."

Joel said, "Sounds like you are feeling scared that she might hurt you again. Staying away is a good way to protect yourself from that."

Sally started to cry. She felt so validated. She hadn't known herself that that was what she was doing, but realized it was true when Joel said it with such loving compassion. Feeling his love put her into her heart, (and a higher level of consciousness) where she started to feel compassion for her sister and herself, "Donna is critical just like my mother was. We both do that. We hated it when our mother did it, but we now do the same thing."

Joel said, "Sounds like you are understanding that she may be scared, too, and doesn't know how to break those old patterns."

Sally said, "I hadn't really thought of it before, but maybe we could talk about it and help each other. We could remind each other when we notice we are doing old stuff and jokingly say, 'Knock it off.' I really don't want to repeat those old patterns. My mom didn't know any better, but maybe we can learn."

In this example, Joel helped Sally find her own solutions by avoiding advice. This often happens when someone feels compassion from another. It is difficult to stay in a low mood when feeling loved, and from a higher mood we have access to our own inner wisdom.

Other people may not find their own solutions. That is not the point. The point is that people can't hear advice from others or their own inner wisdom when they are feeling discouraged. Compassion does not have ulterior motives. People need our compassion even if they stay in a low mood.

Use your feelings compass to recognize a low mood—in yourself and others. This will often transport you immediately out of your low mood and into your heart where you will see and do things from love and inspiration—for yourself and others.

7

The Struggle Can Lead to Understanding

Some people experience a mental struggle when they first hear these principles. Because they habitually use their thought systems to try to figure things out, they can't imagine solving problems any other way. Further, they are used to blaming circumstances for causing their feelings, and are unaccustomed to seeing that it is their way of *thinking about circumstances* that creates their feelings.

Others misinterpret the principles to mean they should quit thinking and become a blob. The opposite is true. Once we truly *understand* the principles, we stop being slaves to our thought system, and thinking as a function becomes our servant. When we are slaves to our thought system, we lack access to the inner wisdom of our heart or spiritual source, thus restricting our perspective and awareness of unlimited possibilities.

We rarely stop thinking, even in our sleep. The point is not to stop thinking, but to understand that *thinking is a function* and that we have the ability to think anything we want, and to use our thinking ability to experience the wonders that come to us from our heart or spiritual source.

Understanding frees us from the prison of our programmed thought system. And yet, a misunderstanding of the principles can lead to increased programming and misuse. I often hear comments like the following:

"I'm afraid to ask a question, or people will know I'm coming from my thought system instead of a higher level of consciousness."

"I still have negative thoughts, so I must not *understand* anything."

"I'm a failure because I yelled at my children. I lost my patience and forgot to come from my heart to see the insecurity behind their behavior."

"I really thought I understood and would not get caught up in my thought system again. The very next day I let myself get hooked into negativity, just like Pavlov's dog. I felt very discouraged and disappointed in myself."

"I just can't feel compassion when my wife drinks, or my husband yells at me, or a friend disappoints me, or things don't turn out the way I want them to. I get angry or upset."

These comments indicate a lack of deeper *understanding,* but it is not helpful to add negative judgment. We do the best we can based on our level of understanding; and we make mistakes on our way to deeper understanding. When we first learn math principles, we make mistakes. As our understanding grows, we make fewer mistakes or use our understanding to correct the mistakes. *Negative judgment only hampers the inspiration that encourages learning.* We can appreciate mistakes when we realize they are simply part of our learning experience. We can enjoy being rosebuds until we become roses in full bloom.

With *understanding,* the concepts of "perfect" and "mistakes" are totally different. Whenever we get upset about mistakes or "not being perfect," we are ego-involved. This simply means we have a *belief* that our self-worth is dependent upon being (or having others be) a certain way. Our expectations do not allow for mistakes. Relax. Life is full of making "mistakes."

Fortunately, little children have no concept of *mistake* when they fall down while learning to walk. They don't waste any time thinking about their fall. If they get hurt, they may cry for a few minutes before getting up and going on.

Thomas Edison was once chided, "It is too bad you had so many failures before you were successful."

Edison replied, "I didn't have failures. I learned many things that did not work."

Understanding the principles helps us recapture that sense of wonder as we journey through life.

By simply giving us a direction or a point of reference on our treasure map, the four principles are like natural laws. The natural law of gravity includes no rule that you should not jump off a building; it simply explains what happens if you do. Similarly, the principle of thought as a function includes no rule that you should not think from your thought system; it simply explains what happens when you do.

Making mistakes in math is not disastrous. It does not even seem like a bother to go back over our figures to find the mistakes and correct them when we feel gratitude for the knowledge allowing us to do that. Knowing how to correct mistakes is simply part of the process. And, for some of us, not knowing how to use calculus does not mean we cannot use addition or subtraction to make our lives easier. In the same way, a lack of deeper understanding of the principles does not keep us from experiencing the benefits of what we do know.

Although airplanes were (before computers) slightly off course more than they were exactly on course, pilots did not waste time fretting, but simply used the principles of navigation to keep getting back on track.

When we see that everything is just as it should be, we see that creating a programmed thought system is perfect—just as an *understanding* of the thought system is perfect. That troublesome thought system can be seen as a wonderful teacher when we acknowledge how many opportunities it gives us to learn wonderful life lessons.

Recently I had thoughts that produced feelings of inadequacy. I found myself wondering, "Will these people like me? Why would they want to spend any time with me?" In the past I would have taken those thoughts seriously and either withdrawn, pretending I didn't care, or would have tried to show off in some way to make them like me. In this instance I noticed the thoughts, dismissed them, and enjoyed myself with the inherent good feelings that arose from my heart. I learned how much I like myself when I dismiss my thought system—and thereby create an energy that is appealing to others. Next time, however, I may forget again, act on thoughts of inadequacy, and not enjoy myself.

The principles let me know when I am on course (because I feel great—or at least aware) and when I am off course. When I am able to dismiss the content of my thinking, I feel grateful. When I do not drop these thoughts, I continue to feel bad—or consciously decide to look for the life lesson.

MIRROR INSIGHT

What if you know all this, yet still can't let go of your negative feelings? Welcome to the club—and to a possibility for seeing your negative feelings as an opportunity to learn more about yourself. Your negative feelings may have a message for you that can provide you with a very important life lesson in order for healing to take place. Look in the mirror and see what there is about *you* that is being reflected by the circumstances you think are causing your negative feelings.

Recently I was on a flight from Germany to Los Angeles. I did not want to check my luggage, a green roll-on case and a small duffle. I stored both pieces in the rack above my seat and settled down to read my novel.

I heard an announcement from a flight attendant that they had a green roll-on case which they would have to put off the plane if it was not claimed. I remember thinking, "That could be mine; I wonder if I should check it out." I dismissed the possibility, however, because I knew my case was stored in the rack. A few minutes before takeoff, I heard my name over the loudspeaker. The two people strapped into their seats next to me had to get up so I could struggle out to the aisle and seek a flight attendant. Another passenger hurried up to me and told me that the man behind me had taken my case out of the rack so he would have room for his things. She was furious because he had left my case in the aisle, and everyone had had to climb over it. I couldn't believe it; but sure enough, when I went to the front of the plane, there was my green suitcase. I explained to the attendant what had happened, but there was not time or space enough to do anything except have my bag checked.

I was so angry at this man that I went back to my seat and confronted him, "What made you think you had the right to take my case out of the rack?" He spoke English very well and calmly explained, "It was above my seat and you are supposed to put your luggage under your seat." (He hadn't bothered to notice that the rack over his seat also extended over my seat.) I couldn't believe it, nor could my fellow passenger who had told me what had happened. She joined me in confronting him. We let him know that we thought he was inconsiderate, selfish, and arrogant. He shrugged it all off as though it were nothing.

I sat in my seat and fumed. I tried to tell myself, "Let it go. This is just your thoughts, and they are driving you crazy. Your anger isn't hurting him, but it is certainly hurting you." I remembered one of my favorite, anonymous quotations: "Anger does more damage to the vessel in which it is stored than to the object upon which it is stored." I also remembered all the scientific research about the damage anger does to the body and to the immune system.

None of that helped. I continued to think about the audacity of this man. I could not understand how he could possibly justify his actions.

After dinner, I met several fellow passengers in the aisle by the restrooms, and they all fed my self-righteousness. One man said, "What a jerk." I loved it. The woman who had already spoken to me said she was still so angry that she couldn't enjoy her meal. I loved it. I went back and told the man off some more.

Can you believe that someone who has written a book on *understanding* could act this way? What about eliminating stress and finding serenity in life and relationships? What about using my feelings as a compass to let me know I was taking my thoughts very seriously?

Well, eventually I did pay attention to my feelings compass, and now I'm thankful to the man who gave me such a wonderful opportunity to learn more about myself and to heal the beliefs that were causing my misery.

I decided to do a meditation and try the mirror insight process to see what my anger was telling me about *myself.* My first glimpse in *the mirror* was to see that I had been a bit (just a bit) selfish and inconsiderate myself to bring two pieces of luggage onto the airplane. If everyone did the same, there wouldn't be enough storage room. It was easy to gloss over my own selfishness when his seemed so much worse.

Notice that last statement. This is the kind of thinking we use often to excuse ourselves from changing. "If someone else is worse, he or she is the one who should change." The truth is that if our fault is not as bad, it should be easier to change. From the thought system, it makes more sense to point fingers instead of changing ourselves. From inner wisdom, we feel humility and drop our judgments.

This small insight, from looking into the mirror, took me into my heart where I felt gratitude to this man for giving me such an excellent opportunity to see myself. Whether or not he was right or wrong for moving my suitcase became a nonissue when I started to understand the message and life lesson my anger had for me. I felt compassion for both of us. I had to laugh at the drama we created from our thought systems. I also felt grateful for the mirror insight process which so often helps me find the gift in every situation.

When we use our feelings compass and discover we are in our thought system, rather than judging or criticizing ourselves, it is helpful to know that every upset provides an opportunity for learning life lessons and healing old programs.

Use your feelings compass to let you know where you are—in your thought system, or in your heart. If this simple awareness does not lead you to an immediate dismissal of your thought system, look in the mirror, find the gifts that can be found in your situation, or seek help to heal your programmed beliefs. One way or another, your feelings compass can point you in the right direction so you can immediately or eventually find your way to your heart.

My present level of understanding has increased the amount of time I live from my heart. I would be foolish to believe the principles are invalid simply because I still sometimes get hooked by my programmed thought system; my understanding is not yet deep enough to save me every time. But my understanding *is* developed enough that I do not take those thoughts as seriously as I used to; I get quiet sooner, or I get help if I need it.

When we get *caught up* in our thought system, it is not helpful to feel guilt or blame or failure. It isn't helpful to fight our thoughts, or to try to control them. This is like trying to control a whirlpool. If we fight and struggle when we get caught in a whirlpool, we will drown; if we relax and get very quiet, it will carry us down, spitting us out the bottom so we can float to the surface. Understanding makes the difference.

Fighting thoughts that make you unhappy is not a life-and-death matter; it is just a matter of happiness or unhappiness. It might take faith to follow suggestions from others who understand the principles that lead to happiness, but once you experience results yourself, you will have access to the wisdom of your own experience.

If you are still struggling with these ideas, it may be that you are trying to understand the principles from your thought system. Your reading this far indicates that your inner wisdom is also *hearing,* in spite of your thoughts. *Understanding* may come from your heart when you least expect it. Not expecting it may mean you have quit thinking about it (quit struggling) so that your inner wisdom and inspiration can surface.

Confusion can be a good sign of progress; it may mean your thought system is being scrambled. This is a good time to drop thought and stop trying to figure it out. Leave room for messages from your heart.

HOW LONG DOES IT TAKE TO UNDERSTAND?

Sometimes *understanding* comes in an instant; sometimes it takes longer. Some people have the impression that *understanding* is an all-or-nothing event, which it can be. It can also be a gradual process of levels of understanding. *Understanding* is actually moment to moment. We may have understanding at one moment, and cover it up with thoughts the next. Or we may have understanding in certain areas and lack understanding in others. In either case, our feelings compass will let us know. When we experience our natural good feelings, we are coming from understanding; when we experience negative emotions, we are coming from our illusions of the past and a lack of understanding of the truth in the present.

For many of us, understanding deepens as we keep listening from our heart. As our understanding deepens, we find more joy and serenity in life.

For me, understanding was not instantaneous. When I first heard these principles, in my heart I knew they were true, but my thought system drove me crazy for a year and a half with objections and questions— "yes, but" and "how about" and "what if." Even though my old thought system kept getting in the way of my understanding, my heart and inner wisdom kept leading me back to hear more, and gradually my "yes, buts" changed to "Of course. It is so simple, so obvious, so wonderful." Before *understanding*, everything can seem heavy and complicated; with *understanding* everything is lighter and simpler.

The learning never ends. Once we get pointed in this direction, life just keeps getting nicer and nicer. Life keeps improving even when there is complete satisfaction with the way things are. George Pransky uses a graphic analogy to explain this phenomenon: It is like waiting at a bus stop for the bus to deeper understanding, but having such a nice time at the bus stop that you don't care if the bus doesn't come. This kind of serenity and satisfaction is found only when we experience life from our heart.

Most people do not experience permanent understanding. We might miss valuable opportunities for continuous learning if we did. It is nice to have at least enough understanding to know, at some level, that there are gifts to be found from the experiences we have when stuck in our thought system. It is nice to have enough understanding that it is difficult to take our thoughts as totally seriously as we would without some level of understanding. It is nice to have enough understanding that we don't judge ourselves or others when we become prisoners of our self-created thought system. Gaining deeper understanding can be seen as an exciting life process leading us to increased experiences of joy and serenity until we are ready for permanent understanding.

SUGGESTIONS

It doesn't matter if you choose not to follow any of the suggestions proposed in this book; their only purpose is to help you see the principles. If you don't see the wisdom behind the suggestions, they will appear to be just more "rules" and "shoulds," and will only create more insecurity, burdens, arguments, or other dissatisfaction. If a suggestion doesn't inspire insight from your inner wisdom, it's all right. Don't *think* about it; just keep *listening* from your heart, and inspired insight will creep up on you when you least expect it.

Suggestions about what to "do" will be meaningful only if you feel confirmation in your heart. When you feel the truth in your heart, the suggestions may trigger your own insight. You may feel something like "Of course! That makes sense, and I know exactly how this applies to my life."

Heart confirmation means you have captured the feeling rather than the words. That feeling may lead you to follow the suggestions in this book (or possibly to do something much different) from your own inner wisdom. You will then be well on your way, because no one knows how to solve your problems better than you do when you dismiss your thought system. The whole point of this book is to help you know that.

Follow the wisdom of your heart, and what to do will be obvious. Your inherent good feelings will guide you to eliminate stress and to find serenity in your life and in your relationships.

8

What Thoughts Are You Willing to Give Up Your Happiness for?

One day I put a nice oak table in the garage for storage. Other family members started putting their junk on the table. I nagged, "Don't put your things on the oak table or it will get scratched." No one listened, and eventually everything from tools and bicycle parts to a worn-out car battery were on the table.

Finally, I went into the garage and cleaned off all the junk so I could cover the table with something to protect it. Sure enough, it was scratched and gouged.

I was angry! Fortunately I had some errands to do, so no one had to listen to me. I drove around, totally lost in my negative thoughts—taking them very seriously.

Finally, my feelings compass let me know that my anger was making me feel upset and miserable. As soon as I became aware of what I was doing to myself with my thoughts, my mood changed. I had to laugh as I began to see things differently.

From our heart, we usually have a wonderful sense of humor. I realized my family had not been irresponsible for putting things on the table; I had been irresponsible by not protecting it in the first place.

Then my insight let me see that I was living my life for scratches in an oak table when there were so many other, much nicer possibilities. It was a beautiful day, and I had been missing it. I had so many things to be grateful for, and I was taking them all for granted. A question came from my inner wisdom, "What thoughts are you willing to give up your happiness for?"

Everyone who hears this story thinks it is funny that I didn't "see the obvious" and have enough sense to cover the table in the first place. This is the point. Silly thinking is usually obvious to anyone who is not caught up in it. When we are caught up in a certain way of interpreting the world, it seems like the only possible reality.

When we are angry, all we see is a world full of bitterness. When we are loving, we see a world full of love, beauty, compassion, forgiveness, gratitude, and peace of mind. *What we think is what we get!*

Go to chapter 4 and look at the Feelings Compass Chart. Thoughts based on any of the concepts in the right column will cause unhappiness. Are any of them worth giving up our happiness for? Any or all of the four principles can lead us back to love and happiness.

WHICH PRINCIPLE IS THE MOST IMPORTANT?

The principles are all interrelated, and any one can come first. Sometimes we will see beauty everywhere because we are in a good mood (a high level of consciousness). Other times, when we are caught up in negative thinking, remembering that thoughts are just thoughts will raise our level of consciousness and we will see things differently.

Sometimes, when we think we are right about something, remembering the fact of separate realities may create humility, and we will then see different realities as interesting rather than as right or wrong. Another time, we may use our feelings as a compass to let us know we are off track. That *understanding* alone may take us out of our thought system and into our heart—or at least tell us we need to get quiet until the thoughts pass and leave room for deeper understanding.

QUIET

Quiet is not necessarily an absence of action, but an absence of negative thoughts running wild in a thought system that takes them seriously. True quiet is not always something that one "does." It may be a feeling of serenity as you go about your daily tasks, or it may be a simple awareness of your thoughts and where they are coming from. Quiet can be enhanced by something you do, such as meditating, walking in nature, or consciously feeling gratitude for the many miracles in your life.

With *understanding,* quiet is natural. Before understanding, it makes sense to actively quiet yourself because slowing down can make it easier to listen to your feelings compass. Getting physically quiet may help you hear the messages from your heart.

Quiet is one of the naturally good feelings we have when we dismiss negative thoughts. If negative thoughts are inspiring frenetic activity *to prove something,* then that activity will also be dismissed, and we will *feel* and *be* more quiet.

Being quiet does not mean sacrificing productivity; instead, we will simply be more selective, from our heart, in what we want to produce. We will also be much more efficient when negative thoughts are not interfering and blinding us to inner wisdom.

Quiet is the humility we feel in the absence of negative thoughts and beliefs. In this quiet and humble state of mind, we have a different experience of life. The world looks very different when seen through feelings of love, gratitude, and compassion—for ourselves and others.

True quiet is total humility—not an attribute of a programmed thought system. Because quiet is such an important path to *understanding,* it is covered more extensively in the next chapter.

THE BRAIN AS A COMPUTER

The brain is like a perfect computer, but it, too, is only as useful as the software put into it and the person's ability to operate it. Using our programmed thought system is the same as using old, outdated software—full of "bugs." It is also the same as trying to operate a computer without understanding the basic principles or reading the instructions. Both produce unsatisfactory results. You are now reading the instructions and gaining an understanding of the principles that can help you eliminate or bypass old, outdated software (the programmed thought system) so you can produce beautiful results in your life.

Many people do not realize that their thoughts and beliefs are not *themselves*, just as software is not the computer. I have seen several versions of a cartoon showing someone smashing a computer because it wouldn't "work" properly. When we take our negative thoughts and beliefs seriously, we are using as much sense as the cartoon character. We have forgotten that it is our thought system that is full of bugs. Our thinking ability is flawless.

Computer buffs know what happens when they try to feed new information into a software program not designed to understand it: The computer beeps and flashes the words "syntax error" on the screen. Even though the new information could improve tremendously the capabilities of the software program, it simply cannot accept the data.

Our brain often does the same thing with new information that could be very useful to us. When we try to filter this information through our thought system, it "beeps" and says, "wrong!" Fortunately, we have something a computer does not have—a heart full of inner wisdom to let us know what new information is useful to improve our lives and relationships, and what information is not useful. We don't have access to the wisdom of the heart, however, until we dismiss the thought system. Dismissing thoughts does not leave a void; it clears the channel so thinking can be used to express heart messages and natural good feelings.

There is a major difference between humans and computers: computers cannot function without software, whereas humans function best without their thought systems. Another major difference is how software is programmed.

SOFTWARE (PROGRAMMED THOUGHT SYSTEM)

Computer software is written by people with knowledge of computer language. The computer industry is mushrooming as knowledge increases and applications multiply. Old software is thrown out as improved software is designed. Wouldn't it be wonderful if we could throw out our old software when it becomes outdated? Actually that is just what happens when we dismiss our thought system and live from our heart. However, there is a reason we sometimes don't do this, or that it doesn't always last when we do.

Unfortunately, the largest portion of our programmed thought system is created when we are very young and lacking in knowledge. Much of our program comes from the decisions we make (thoughts and beliefs we create) in response to the parenting methods we experienced. (This is not meant to blame parents, but to understand the process of how a thought system is created.)

In our parenting workshops we point out that children are always making decisions (at a subconscious level) about who they are, what the world is like, and what they need to do (how they need to behave) in this world to thrive or to survive. Since many of these decisions are made based on a child's fear of disapproval and/or punishment, many decisions have to do with surviving instead of thriving. This may have made sense when we were children. The problem is that we hang on to these decisions when they no longer serve us.

Valerie Seeman Moreton describes this process in her book, *Heal the Cause:*

> Anytime we make a decision with great emotion attached, it becomes the subconscious "rule of action" from that time forth. This means that when an upset occurs, even at a very young age, like one or two, a decision is made (subconsciously) that influences the rest of your life. If that decision was that you were "not loved" or "not good enough," your whole life would be about compensating for that belief to prove it was false. Behaving in a particular way to get love or approval can cause self-defeating patterns to develop and defense mechanisms to

87

form. And all of this is based upon a lie, founded upon fear instead of love.[1]

Many defense mechanisms take the form of mis-behavior. Through experiential activities, adults gain understanding about how the thought system is formed—theirs and their children's. They also learn that the best way to help a "misbehaving child" change beliefs and behavior is through love (encouragement), not fear (punishment). Love can take both parent and child out of their thought system and into their heart where effective solutions can be found.

As adults, we also "misbehave" when fear creates defense mechanisms. We don't experiece fear when we access our heart or spiritual souce. Fear comes only from the illusions of old programming in the thought system. When we have difficulty "throwing away" old, outdated programming, it could be that subconscious decisions and beliefs have not been brought into awareness and healed. It could be that we have not yet learned the life lesson or seen the gifts that can be found in our situation. Learning the lesson (seeing the gift) can immediately take you out of your thought system and into your heart.

SEEING THE LESSONS

There are many master teachers and scientists who teach us that there is divine order to everything. Per-

[1]Valerie Seeman Moreton, N.D., *Heal the Cause* (San Diego: Kalos Publishing, 1996).

haps shifting back and forth from our thought system and heart increases our appreciation for happiness and peace of mind. Perhaps we could not learn important life lessons any other way.

Not long ago, I was using my thought system in a way that was making me miserable. Because I thought a friend was being inconsiderate, I was upset; my stomach was churning and I couldn't sleep. When my feelings compass let me know what I was doing, I clearly saw that I was giving up my happiness for some negative thoughts. My awareness was followed by a message from my heart inviting me to look in the mirror and see the lessons I could learn from my experience: *Which is worse, being inconsiderate, or being judgmental?* I had to laugh at my self-righteousness. Then I saw that it was not even a matter of being better or worse, because being inconsiderate and judgmental are both simply aspects of thought-provoked insecurity from a programmed thought system.

Perspective and compassion quickly followed as I remembered the many times I have been inconsiderate either because I didn't know better, or because I *believed* I was justified. I also realized that just because I *thought* this friend was being inconsiderate didn't mean she was; it meant only that she was not living up to some rules and beliefs *I had created* from my programmed thought system. I laughed at those thoughts also, and could then feel love and gratitude for my friend—and for myself. I had learned, again, that there are not any thoughts I am willing to give up my happiness for.

When happiness is more important to you than anything else, you will be happy, because there will be no thoughts for which you will be willing to give up your happiness for. You will do whatever it takes to get out of your thought system and into your heart.

9

Quiet

An *understanding* of the principles can lead to quiet, or quiet can lead to an *understanding* of the principles. It has been mentioned often that getting quiet is an excellent way to dismiss the thought system, or at least to wait patiently until it loses its hold over you.

Getting quiet can mean many things. It can mean simply staring out the window, taking a nap, reading a book, or anything that distracts you from the busyness of your programmed thought system. Another way to get quiet is through meditation.

Meditation can lead to the ultimate quiet for some people (going into "the silence," or "the gap between thoughts"). For others, meditation may be a time to sit quietly as a simple exercise in an awareness of the busy thought system, for deep relaxation, or to listen to messages or inspiration from their heart or spiritual source.

MEDITATION

For years I wanted to meditate, but thought I couldn't do it. Every time I tried to meditate in groups, I would either go to sleep, or my legs would twitch, or I just couldn't make my mind get quiet. When I tried to meditate by myself, it drove me crazy to sit for five minutes, let alone twenty. I just couldn't do it. Listen to that language. I "couldn't"? Well, it sure seemed that way.

I now meditate for at least twenty minutes almost every day. How did I get from there to here? It took commitment based on my understanding of the importance of a quiet mind to access my heart and my spiritual source. Because of this commitment, I took three weeks out of my life to go to a wonderful retreat. While there, I made the commitment to sit for twenty minutes—no matter what. I was prepared to listen to the chatter of my mind for twenty minutes if that's all that happened.

The first day I was peeking at my watch every five minutes. The second day I went fifteen minutes before I peeked. But instead of feeling energized, as I had been led to expect, I found that I was totally wiped out. So, I took a nap. The third day, I scheduled a walk into nature after my meditation so I could wake up. By the fourth or fifth day, I stopped peeking at my watch, and meditation began to feel wonderful.

I gave up all my expectations (except for my commitment to sit for twenty minutes), and then all my expectations started to happen. That may sound like double-talk, but I now know that not being attached to expectations allows them room to happen—or not. And that is what my meditations are like. Sometimes I receive profound messages from my heart or spiritual source. Other times I simply feel love and comfort. Simply! The chatter of my mind comes and goes. I just let it be. (Well, sometimes, when the chatter gets too aggravating, I may take deep breaths or concentrate on love and gratitude.)

Meditation is a wonderful way to get quiet if you leave your expectations and judgments behind. It can be a vehicle that takes you to your heart or spiritual source. During this time of quiet, you may simply be aware of your thoughts. You may experience your inherent good feelings of love, gratitude, and joy. You may receive inspiration or specific messages regarding a life concern.

During one of my meditations, I received the following message: *What is insight except sight from within? Walking through life without insight from your heart and your spiritual source is like walking through life with your eyes closed.*

On my next nature walk, I tried walking with my eyes closed. Try it sometime. Find a path where there are no other people, if you can, and try walking with your eyes closed. What happens? Do you feel fear, mistrust, disorientation, insecure? How long can you keep going before you have to open your eyes? Remember, this is on a path where there are no other distractions. What happens when you try walking with your eyes closed on a busy sidewalk or on a busy street? I realized that I am usually going through life thinking my eyes are wide open, when in truth my thoughts have created many illusions that distract me from my inner peace and produce fear, mistrust, disorientation, and insecurity. I am literally *in the dark*. *Understanding* the principles is like turning on the light. Quiet through meditation can facilitate *understanding*.

Those who say they don't have time to meditate is saying they don't have time to open the eyes of their heart—that they would prefer to go through life in the dark.

How much of the movie do you see when the video is on fast forward? Living your life without meditation is like keeping the VCR on fast forward. You are missing the movie of your life. Put the video on pause, take time for meditation, and see how much more present you will be in the story of your own life.

CHORE MEDITATION

You can experience a state of meditation without sitting quietly. You can bring a state of meditation into your daily living.

Think of a chore you'd rather not do—for example, washing the dishes. Take a deep breath and quiet your mind. Then wash the dishes with love. Avoid rushing. Be fully in the moment and bring joy to every movement. Then bring your gratitude to the task. It is amazing how much you can find to be grateful for: the nourishing food you ate, the wonderful invention of running water, your nice dishes. Be grateful for this opportunity to bring a state of meditation into everything you do.

NATURE

Quiet can be enhanced in nature. We need nature in our lives to ground us, to nurture us, to give us messages (yes, nature will talk with you—more about that later), and to bring us to joy and gratitude.

We all love to be in nature, whether it be in a park, on the ocean, in the mountains, or near a stream, lake, or pond. We all feel rejuvenated and renewed in those special places. We feel relaxed and peaceful. Yet most of our time in life is spent in our busy-ness away from nature. In fact, some people take their busy minds with them when they go into nature and rob themselves of nature's soothing energy.

For those who live in an urban environment, taking the time to be in nature is essential. Likewise, those who live in more rural areas need to take the time to appreciate the beauty and simplicity of nature that surrounds them, instead of taking it for granted.

Do you remember those times as a child when you would spend hours fascinated with one miracle of nature after another? Remember the times you would watch a bird in flight and wonder what it would feel like to fly, or lie for hours on a grassy hillside and watch clouds take all kinds of shapes? Can you remember how fascinating it was to watch a spider spin its web, or to watch how the ants were so intent with purpose and order in their work? You may have marveled at the beauty of a plant or flower and just immersed yourself in the scent of it. And the ocean: Can you remember marveling at the vastness of that body of water and the immense power it has—and your joy as you played with the waves, or your contentment as you built a sand castle?

Try taking your childlike wonder back into nature. Take time to watch it, and feel it, and enjoy it. Many of us have simply forgotten about the importance of nature and how it truly feeds us to our core. Is that busyness of everyday living so important that we don't even have enough time to feed ourselves properly? We need to examine our priorities. Sometimes old platitudes are worth remembering—are we taking time to smell the roses?

One way to become more aware of how to connect with the earth and nature is to learn what the history of Native Americans has to teach us. The Native Americans were completely connected with nature. They lived off the land just as the animals do. They knew the uses of all the plants and animals, and had respect and a feeling of gratitude for what the earth, their mother, was providing for them. Showing respect and reverence for the earth, nature, and the animals that provided them with food was part of their sacred rituals.

Many of us, and our children, have completely lost touch with the joys of nature. Many years ago, my family and I rented a camper and went to Sequoia National Park for a week. For the first two days the children were miserable. They were devastated that they couldn't watch television. They complained that there was nothing to do. We tried to convince them that there was plenty to do out in the woods, but that possibility seemed beyond their comprehension.

Eventually, however, they became bored with boredom and began to poke their heads outside. It wasn't long before they heard the call of nature. They played in the streams, climbed trees, created huts in the woods, gathered wood for the fire pit, went on hikes, played games with sticks and rocks, and chased squirrels. They were so alive. At the end of the week, they didn't want to leave.

There is an important lesson for all of us in the experience of these children. Nature is calling to all of us who are willing to listen. Our lives are enriched tremendously when we leave technology and our busy minds behind and take time to spend in and with nature.

Everyone can find a place to go and commune with nature. It could be a city park, the beach, the woods, the desert, or anywhere in the countryside. Find a rock to sit on, a tree to lean on, or grass to lie on and let yourself be open to the nurturing energy of nature. Be open to messages you can receive from the wind and the sun. Sometimes you may want to ask a tree, a rock, a leaf, or any part of nature what message it has for you. Take a notepad and pencil so you can record the message.

At workshops I have shared this possibility with many people.[1] When I explain the exercise, some say I must be kidding. But when they come back after doing the exercise they are humbled. The insights

---

[1] I was first introduced to this exercise in a workshop with Jack and Deborah Bartello. For information on their workshops call 800-446-5959.

they have gained into themselves and the messages they have received are truly inspiring. As they read their messages to each other we sometimes have to pass the Kleenex box, for people are truly moved, and often see how the message someone else received is also helpful to themselves.

You might experience personal benefit from the following messages one person found in nature:

Message from a Stump

I am a tree stump—being what I am.
I don't care about judgments of others.
Some may say I don't have the magnificence of
    the tall, strong tree I once was,
But it doesn't matter.
Part of me was chopped down and hauled
    away—for some good use, I am sure.
I am still beautiful.
Look at my patterns—in my bark, in my bare
    wood.
    —in the niches and crevices where bugs find
    refuge.
You may stand on me, or sit on me and bask in
    the sun.

My message to you about love: There is nothing
    to be except who you are.
Look closely and see the beauty of who you are.

You might enjoy keeping a "nature messages" journal. Write down the messages you receive from different parts of nature. One day it may be a tree. Another day it may be a leaf, a raindrop, a twig, a pond, a mountain, sand, or a rock. The possibilities are endless—as are the messages.

SPIRITUAL MESSAGES EVERYWHERE

Spiritual messages can also be found in everything that happens to you. For example, on my walk one morning I was listening to some music on my small tape player. The earphones started to buzz. I wondered what the spiritual message could be. It was so obvious: *Your mind is buzzing away all the time. Don't let it interfere. Just let it be and enjoy the music. You don't have to make your thoughts go away. Just don't give them so much energy and other information will get through.* An amazing thing happened. The buzzing in the earphones stopped. Another amazing thing happened. My buzzing thoughts didn't stop. I'm joking, of course—it's not at all amazing that my thoughts kept buzzing. They never stop. But how nice to know that I don't have to pay so much attention to them.

When we are open to spiritual messages, they can be found anytime we are willing to receive them.

Let's tackle a seemingly difficult situation. Suppose someone with whom you think you are very much in love leaves you. What kind of spiritual message could there possibly be in that? Could it be that there is something better in store for you?—perhaps a better relationship, or perhaps an occasion to learn how much you can enjoy being by yourself? Or could it be that your spiritual source knows it is not good for you to be with this person?

We have all heard stories about people who believed that someone's abandoning them was the worst thing that could ever happen to them, until time passed (sometimes years) and they came to see that the leaving was the *best* thing that could have happened to them.

We can't hear these message when we give more credibility to our egos and programmed beliefs than we do to our spiritual source. And that is okay. We are ready when we are ready.

If you aren't ready to see spiritual messages in so-called catastrophic events, start with less emotional events. Suppose you are taking a walk and you come to a big hill. You are tired and *think* you can't make it. Tune in to the message from the hill. The first question you might ask is, "Do I really *want* to climb this hill?" Maybe it is time to turn around and go in another direction. If you do want to climb the hill, you may get other messages, such as, "Slow down. What's the hurry? Take time to rest. Go one step at a time. Pause and look at the beautiful scenery all around you." Another message could be that the difficult climb will strengthen your muscles and help you become more fit. Then comes the fun part. Notice how all those messages may fit perfectly in your life. Focus on a life problem you are having. See if any of the messages would be helpful.

APPRECIATION WALKS

Try an appreciation walk. Tune in with appreciation and gratitude for everything you see. Sometimes your focus may be close to the ground. Other times you may focus on horizons and vistas. You may be drawn to focus on birds or other animals. Notice the breezes or wind, the sun, or any sounds of nature. You may focus on short distances, long distances, or anywhere in between. Notice how much there is to see and appreciate. See how long you can go before you lose your focus on nature and become distracted by the busy-ness of your mind. Do not judge yourself or anything that happens, just become aware.

SELF-DEFEATING BELIEFS AND BEHAVIORS

In her book, *A Return to Love*, Marianne Williamson confirms what happens when we forget that we created our own thought system and ego.

Not everyone chooses to heed the call of his own heart. As all of us are only too aware, the loud and frantic voices of the outer world easily drown out the small still loving voice within.[2]

Many of us who seek quiet use the ego of our thought system to defeat ourselves in many ways. Four ways to consider are expectations, self-defeating judgments, lack of awareness, and not seeing the gift in all things.

[2]Marriane Williamson, *A Return to Love* (New York: Harper Paperbacks, 1992), p. 67.

Expectations

George had a great meditation. He felt connected to his soul. He felt love and joy. The energy was so strong that he walked around in bliss for a day. The next morning he meditated and was very disappointed. His experience was nothing like the day before. He spent the rest of that day in total depression. What had happened?

George's expectations got in the way. He wanted his second meditation to be just like the first. George wasn't aware of it, but his expectations had become part of his programmed thought system.

Self-Defeating Judgments

Then George allowed his judgments to take over. He beat up on himself for not having a "high enough" level of consciousness to meditate "right." He compared himself to others who surely had better meditation experiences than he did—all the time.

Lack of Awareness

Of course, he wasn't aware that it was his *expectations* and *judgments* that were creating blocks. If he had been so aware, his judgments would have been defused and he could be open to his heart. Judgments can't take over unless we let them. We let them when we forget that they don't have a life of their own—we create them. Awareness leads to understanding, or understanding leads to awareness. We can then be open to seeing the gift in all things.

Not Seeing the Gift in All Things

George had heard about seeing the gift in all things. The third day he sat in meditation and asked his heart to show him the gift in what he was experiencing. He soon received an insight about his expectations and his judgments—and he laughed. He then realized how often he let his expectations and his judgments keep him from seeing the gifts in his life experiences. He still did not have the same experience as his meditation on the first day, but he didn't compare them. He felt total joy in what he did experience.

Another message that came to him was, *What is, IS.* He had heard that before, but now it had new meaning for him. He knew that on some days he may not receive any messages at all, but that sitting quietly during his meditation time would be enough—a beautiful gift. When he felt blocked, he would tune into the blocks and see if they had anything to teach him.

Sometimes it seems as though our minds and messages from the world were created solely to take us away from our heart and spiritual experiences. They were and they weren't, depending on your perspective. From our heart we can see that the world and our minds give us many opportunities to strengthen our spiritual experience. The sooner we can see the gift in all things, the sooner we experience love and gratitude.

GLIMPSES ARE ENOUGH

It seems to be the human condition to spend more time experiencing life through our programmed though systems than from our hearts. While we are learning it is helpful to appreciate the glimpses. Every glimpse into *understanding* is like money in the bank that we can draw on when we need it.

While writing this book, I had a huge glimpse into the serenity and peace of mind that comes from *understanding*. I felt so loving and such joy and gratitude, it seemed that nothing could disturb my peace.

I was given a big test. I had paid a typesetter over $1,000, in advance, to complete a revision of one of my self-published books. One day I dropped by to see how she was doing. I learned that the company had gone into some kind of bankruptcy and that someone from the court system came by every day to collect their daily receipts. Part of the bankruptcy agreement was that they had to collect a certain amount of money to hand over to the court or they would lose their business completely. So, they would work on projects where they could collect money when they were finished—instead of projects where the money had been received in advance and was long gone. My friends and family could hardly believe how undisturbed I was by this news. I honestly believed it would all turn out for the best—even if I lost the money. From this state of mind, I discussed the situation very calmly and lovingly with the woman who was working on the typesetting. I did not blame her or get angry with her. I empathized with her and the conditions under which she had to work.

She stayed late and worked on her own time to finish my project. She later told me that my energy was so encouraging to her that she wanted to do all she could to help me.

I wish I could say I was able to stay in that state of mind. I have since let other situations disturb my peace. However, that experience is "in the bank." I love to remember it and draw on its energy as a reminder that, no matter what happens, I have a choice to deal with any situation from love or from fear.

Glimpses are truly wonderful gifts. Be gentle with yourself while you are strengthening your *understanding*, and be gentle while you are learning to get quiet and hear the messages from your heart.

10

Contrary to Popular Opinion

Our programmed thought system is full of many beliefs that block the inner wisdom, inspiration, and natural good feelings inherent from our heart. Therefore, when we have access to our heart, we often see things differently from the mainstream of popular opinion. One of the beliefs perpetuated by popular opinion is that we need rules to live by.

RULES

As our understanding deepens, we realize that when living from our heart or spiritual source we need no rules. Rules are based on thoughts that create fear. Some people fear that without rules anarchy would prevail—rape, murder, lying, cheating, and stealing.

This is not true. Most people would not consider inhumane acts even if there were no laws prohibiting them. And people who do are not stopped by laws. Thought-produced insecurity creates negative behavior. People enjoying their inner wisdom do positive things naturally—without rules.

When our heart is blocked, we fail to listen as our inner wisdom tries to get through and tell us, "This rule does not make sense." If we would listen, we would see that the rule is often based on judgments of right and wrong instead of love and encouragement. We usually ignore this inner guidance, hearing instead our thoughts saying, "You are not following this rule well enough." We then feel inadequate, frustrated, depressed, and more insecure, creating a vicious cycle.

It makes no sense to rely on rules when we have access to our inner wisdom and inspiration. As our heart guides us through each day, we will experience positive results and enjoy life. It will not lead us astray.

Although much of what I have been teaching may sound like rules, there is a great difference between principles and rules. A principle is like a road map: It does not include rules about where we *should* go, but lets us know where we are, or where we will end up, depending on which direction we travel. If we are in Virginia and want to go to New York, it makes no sense to go south. Likewise, if we are feeling bad, and want to feel good, it makes no sense to use our thought system and take our negative thoughts seriously.

By turning any of the examples or suggestions into rules, we make them a part of our thought system, changing them beyond the recognition of our inner wisdom. They are no longer principles. Rules are like "shoulds," with a sense of punishment and reward attached. Principles are natural laws, which simply let us understand the natural consequences of what we do.

When we listen from our heart, we *hear* principles rather than rules.

DOING

What we do is a direct result of our state of mind. When we allow our natural good feelings to surface (by dismissing negative thoughts), our state of mind is one of love, gratitude, and compassion. In this happy state of mind, we have access to inspiration, common sense, and wisdom. What we do from a happy state of mind will therefore be different from what we do in the state of mind we create through the filters of our thought system.

When we are nice because we think that is how we "should" behave, there will be a nagging dissatisfaction. Often there are strings attached—expectations such as, "If I am nice, then things should turn out my way," or, "then people will love me." The world looks and feels different when we get beyond our thought system. When we are nice because it feels like the natural thing to do, we will experience satisfaction and contentment. There are no strings attached. There is true joy in the doing. Receiving love doesn't seem to be an issue; we find so much pleasure in loving.

Sometimes we feel inspired to do something nice, but our thoughts sneak in and turn it into a "should." We will know this has happened when our feelings change from peaceful to stressed and anxious, or resentful. A friend shared how this had happened to her. She said she loves baking cookies for friends and family during the holidays, but one year she realized it was no longer fun because she felt she *should* bake cookies for what had become a long list of people. What she had started from her heart crossed over to her thought system, and the joy was gone.

A FAIRY TALE

Once upon a time there were two fairy princesses, Princess Dew and Princess Bee.

Princess Dew was very busy running around doing things for other people, trying to make them happy. Some people loved what Princess Dew did for them, but instead of being happy, they just wanted more. Princess Dew tried hard to do more for them, hoping that someday they would be happy. Other people did not like what she did for them "for their own good" and wished she would stop interfering.

Princess Dew became worn out, bitter, and frustrated because people did not appreciate all she did for them. She was very unhappy. No one wanted to be around her.

Princess Bee was also very busy—being happy. She enjoyed everything: rainbows and clouds, rainy days and sunny days. She especially enjoyed people. She loved watching them "be." People loved being around her. Her happiness was contagious.

SERVICE

The fairy tale of Princess Bee and Princess Dew is not meant to suggest that we should not do things for others. A happy state of mind will probably inspire us to be of service to others in any way we can. What we do, however, will not come from shoulds or ulterior motives, and it will not be conditional. Service will be for the joy of the moment.

We will also know when to be of service to ourselves. Taking care of ourselves is not selfish when it is inspired from our inner wisdom. The greatest thing we can do for ourselves and our relationships is to take care of ourselves and to *be happy*.

SELFISHNESS

It is popular to have strong negative opinions about selfishness, and, in fact, the self-centeredness that comes from the thought system looks and feels like the popular descriptions. The self-interest that comes from inner wisdom and a happy state of mind, however, has a different look and feel.

I know this sounds like double-talk—until you see the difference, which is in the feeling. Selfishness from the thought system is based on ego, self-importance, resentment, rebellion, or total disregard for others; self-interest from a natural, happy state of mind is based on feelings of love and the joy of living. With these feelings, we will want to do whatever our inner wisdom leads us to do to enjoy life.

Because of our old beliefs about selfishness, we could let our thought system convince us that doing what we want is "selfish." If we stick to following the feeling from our inner wisdom, however, we will know the difference—no matter what anyone else thinks.

One day Mary felt like going for a nice, long walk. She received a message from her thought system: "You should not go for a walk when you have so many other things to do, like cleaning the house and shopping." She dismissed her thoughts and listened to her heart. She went for a walk and enjoyed the beautiful day. Her family came home to a happy wife and mother. They enjoyed being around her and felt her love.

Martha also wanted to go for a walk, but she listened to the shoulds from her thought system. She felt depressed and did not get much cleaning done. Her family came home to an unhappy wife and mother.

If you are asking, "How will anything ever get done if we always do what we want instead of doing what really needs to be done?" you have missed the point. The next day Martha went for a walk, but still felt depressed. Mary stayed home and cleaned house, and still felt happy.

From a happy feeling, Mary is able to know what is important for her own well-being and that of her family. From an unhappy feeling, Martha will feel dissatisfied no matter what she does. For example,

Martha has trouble getting her children to do their chores, while Mary has inspiration for how to win the cooperation of her children. When Mary cleans house, it is because she enjoys a clean house, not because she is compulsive, or following shoulds. When Martha cleans house she is trying to prove that she is a good wife and mother.

When we enjoy a nice life, we will be creating serenity in our home, and in the world.

Happiness and peace of mind are contagious.

DECISIONS

Contrary to common belief, it is not helpful to figure things out or make decisions when feeling stress. This only keeps us deeply enmeshed in our thought system. It is as ineffective as keeping our foot on the gas pedal to get out of a ditch, while the spinning wheel digs deeper and deeper into the sand.

If you have any doubts about what to do, or want to do something because of negative feelings such as anger, let that be your clue that you are lost in your thought system. Get quiet and wait for your negative feelings to pass so your inner wisdom can surface.

Decisions from our heart are always positive and produce good results. We know when decisions are inspiration from our inner wisdom and need not doubt their appropriateness.

Actually, the concept of decision changes with understanding. The familiar concept of decision implies choice or effort. With understanding, decisions feel more like obvious, common-sense things to do than like choices or efforts.

Deepak Chopra discusses this as "The Law of Least Effort," the fourth of *The Seven Spiritual Laws of Success.*

> Least effort is expended when your actions are motivated by love, because nature is held together by the energy of love. When you seek power and control over other people, you waste energy. When you seek money or power for the sake of the ego, you spend energy chasing the illusion of happiness instead of enjoying happiness in the moment. When you seek money for personal gain only, you cut off the flow of energy to yourself, and interfere with the expression of nature's intelligence. But when your actions are motivated by love, there is no waste of energy. When your actions are motivated by love, your energy multiplies and accumulates— and the surplus energy you gather and enjoy can be channeled to create anything that you want, including unlimited wealth.[1]

Recently I was trying to make a decision about how to handle a situation where I felt treated unjustly by someone. I thought I had made some progress because of my willingness to take responsibility for how I had helped create the situation. I knew I was still in my thought system, however, because I wanted to confront

---

[1]Deepak Chopra, *The Seven Spiritual Laws of Success* (San Rafael: Amber-Allen Publishing & New World Library, 1994).

this person, tell him how I felt, and let him know I was going to make sure I did not invite unjust treatment anymore. This decision did not create good feelings.

I decided to get quiet and meditate for a while. The understanding that I was in my thought system allowed me to dismiss the thoughts and listen for wisdom from my heart. It didn't take long for me to receive a message. *Are you going to use love power or anger power? Sharing your feelings from love will be much more effective than sharing them from anger. There will be no sense of blame. You will simply practice what you preach about identifying a problem and finding a solution. Taking responsibility is much more effective from love than from anger.*

Once again, I had seen how easy it is to make rules out of wisdom. I had seen the wisdom of taking responsibility for how I contribute to situations. In this situation I was doing this as a rule, and it didn't help me feel better. As soon as I used my feelings compass to find that I was in my thought system, I was open for fresh inspiration from my heart.

A decision may make sense in one situation. If we make a rule out of it, however, we will lose touch with our inner wisdom and inspiration. No matter how similar the situation is, it may call for a completely different decision at another time. Only our inner wisdom can let us know.

INTELLIGENCE

Joe commented to Zeke, "I'd rather be smart and miserable than a happy fool."

Wise old Zeke asked, "Is that smart?"

Some people believe that it is a sign of intelligence to find fault and ugliness in the world; they call it being realistic and think anyone who can't see the negativity as they do is being a blind fool. Of course, these people are not happy when they are being negative.

I prefer a definition of intelligence that includes the wisdom to be happy, no matter what other people think.

PATIENCE

"I just lost my patience," claimed Helen.

"If only I could be more patient," sighed Henry.

And so the struggle goes when people believe patience is a matter of self-control, or a quality that must be developed. Patience is natural when we experience life through our heart and feel full of peace and contentment.

Impatience is created from thoughts of dissatisfaction, expectation, or judgment. Dismiss those thoughts and you have patience, because it is impossible to feel impatient and satisfied at the same time.

You may ask, "How can I possibly be patient when someone is doing something I know they shouldn't be doing?" Turning the other cheek always seemed terribly wimpy to me. It makes sense now. When we see the innocence in what others do from a lack of understanding, it makes no sense to lash out at them or to lose our own peace of mind in reaction to their insecurity. It does make sense to create a loving, forgiving atmosphere in which they can best gain

116

understanding, or to know when they are not ready to learn.

FORGIVENESS

An unwillingness to forgive is one of the greatest blocks to our inner wisdom. It is based on ego, judgments, self-righteousness, lack of compassion, and a belief that there is only one possible reality—mine!

The ego has some very powerful hooks. Being "right" is a huge one. For many of us, being right wins over love and peace most of the time. Being right can take many forms. Sometimes we feel we have a *right* to feel miserable. After all, look what those people (our parents) or that person (boss, spouse, friend) did to us. "I would much rather feel miserable about that than to let go and feel love and peace. That would mean I would have to let go of all my judgments and feel compassion—and (gulp) even forgiveness." There is only one thing to be gained by not forgiving—misery!

People who have the popular opinion that forgiveness is something you have to work at or try to do are engrossed in ego and judgment. It is self-righteous to think, "Well, I know you did something wrong, but I will be big enough to forgive you." Or, "You did a despicable thing, and you don't deserve forgiveness." Lack of forgiveness harms the unforgiving more than the unforgiven. It is impossible to be happy while holding on to judgments.

Anyone who says, "I will forgive, but I won't forget," doesn't understand forgiveness: Forgiveness *is* forgetting. It is realizing that ego, expectations, and judgments are thoughts that are not worth hanging on to, and, when we let go of them, they are forgotten. Dismissing negative thoughts and forgiving are synonymous.

Forgiveness is natural from a level of consciousness that includes compassion, love, humor, gratitude, and peace of mind. Forgiveness is not even an issue when we have these feelings, because when we see with *understanding*, there is nothing to forgive.

CIRCUMSTANCES

Contrary to popular opinion, circumstances have nothing to do with happiness. As we have discussed, our thoughts about circumstances create our state of mind.

We often hear people say things like, "I'll be happy when I finish school"; ". . . when I'm married"; ". . . when I'm single"; ". . . when I have more money"; ". . . when I have children"; or, ". . . when you do what I want you to do."

If you are not happy before you get what you want, you won't be happy after you get it. People who think they are happy when they first get what they want find that happiness doesn't last long. When things settle down they feel that old, nagging insecurity and dissatisfaction, or they get trapped back in their feelings of unhappiness the first time things don't go the way they think they should.

During a discussion of these principles, one man asked, "Do you mean to tell me that losing my legs would not be a reason for me to be unhappy?"

He was told, "That is right. It is only what you could think about losing your legs that could create unhappiness."

He replied, "That is the most stupid thing I ever heard of."

Another man who was listening spoke up, "It is true. I lost both my legs in Vietnam, but I have never been happier. That does not mean I don't wish I had my legs. I would love to have my legs back, but before I learned about these principles, I didn't know how to be happy when I had them. Now I know how to be happy even without them."

Happiness is a state of mind that allows us to see things differently. In a happy state of mind (from our heart) we see life with gratitude and a different perspective. Circumstances look different when seen through the filter of our thought system.

Happiness is a state of mind that comes from *within.*

You may be wondering, "But what about things that are beyond my control, like sickness or negative things other people do?" When we have peace of mind and contentment, we see *what is* without judgment, like the wise man in the following story.

A HORSE STORY

Many years ago, a wise man lived in an old mountain village. One day a beautiful, wild stallion ran into his corral. When the villagers heard the news, they came to his farm and marveled, "What a wonderful thing! You are so fortunate!"

The wise man replied, "Maybe so, maybe not."

A few days later the stallion broke the corral fence and ran away. When the villagers heard the news, they came to his farm and said, "What a terrible thing! What bad luck!"

The wise man replied, "Maybe so, maybe not."

The next day the stallion returned, bringing a whole herd of mares. When the villagers heard the news, they came and exclaimed, "Now you are the richest man in the village, and surely the luckiest!"

The wise man replied, "Maybe so, maybe not."

The wise man's son tried to break one of the mares, but was thrown and broke his leg. When the villagers heard the news, they came and sympathized, "What a tragedy! Who will help you now with the harvest? This is such a misfortune!"

The wise man replied, "Maybe so, maybe not."

The next day the Cossacks came to get all the young men of the village to fight in their wars. They did not take the wise man's son because of his broken leg.

SEEING WHAT IS WITHOUT JUDGMENT

You may ask, "But what if I'm not in a state of mind that allows me to see things without judgment? What if I do have negative thoughts and feelings about external circumstances?"

The most helpful thing is to accept yourself and have compassion for yourself as you are—without judgment. When we are confronted with circumstances we can't seem to understand and we add negative thoughts to them, we have two things we dislike—the circumstances and our negative thoughts about them. Our thoughts are usually much worse than the circumstances, and it is our thoughts that produce our feelings.

We don't see the beauty of life or experience feelings of joy and gratitude when we waste time and energy on judgments. Judgments fill us with toxic feelings.

A good example is the story of two men who lost their fortunes. One was distraught about his circumstances and jumped off a building. The other man saw them as an opportunity to start over again in something new. (As you might expect, the man who jumped off the building was not a happy person even when he had his fortune, whereas the man who saw the opportunity had been enjoying life during all of his varied circumstances.)

Some argue, "I can understand how that applies to most circumstances, but not to others." People will often think of extreme cases to prove a principle invalid, instead of simply applying the principle to situations in their own lives, where they would know it is true.

I have found that as I experience the principles in areas where I do not doubt, my understanding deepens. I then doubt less and see the principles in areas I had formerly been unable to understand. This is a progression that never ends. Understanding keeps deepening, and life keeps appearing more beautiful. Actually, life *is* always beautiful. We either see it, or we don't.

11

Detours

There are many detours that keep us from accessing the natural good feelings and wisdom of our heart. All of these detours come from the old perceptions and beliefs that have formed our programmed thought system.

INSECURITY

Even though insecurity is just another thought, it can be very powerful when taken seriously. Every negative act is based on thoughts that produce insecurity. The insecurity may be at a subconscious level, but it is followed by each individual's interpretations of what he or she needs to do to compensate. Thought-provoked insecurity may appear in the form of aggressiveness, shyness, drug abuse, self-righteousness, the need to prove one's worth through achievements, or feelings of inadequacy.

Many positive acts also are motivated by insecurity from the thought system. Pleasers (approval junkies) do loving things for others to "buy" love. Powermongers may engage in positive actions to serve their purposes. (I won't even go into politics.) From our heart, we won't judge these acts, but we will *understand*.

Insecurity may lead us to adopt the belief system of someone else, or to imagine they are the source of our wisdom. This is especially dangerous when we follow a guru because we hear beautiful words of wisdom and don't listen to our own inner wisdom. This is not the intention of many gurus. They keep telling us the truth is within. Other so-called "gurus" gather followers to form cults. And when teenagers cave in to peer pressure, they relinquish their ability to listen to their inner wisdom. What a difference it could make for them to *understand* the four principles.

EGO AND SELF-IMPORTANCE

The illusion of insecurity is strongly connected with the illusions of ego and proving self-importance. It is impossible to find happiness through trying to prove self-importance. Temporary relief might be found through some kind of achievement, but it doesn't last.

When you get off track into your thought system, notice how often the detour is related to proving your self-importance. It is strenuous just to think about all the antics we go through in life to prove something that has no need to be proven.

The ego is the strongest part of the thought system. It works very hard to protect itself. It is not at all interested in being dismissed and replaced by your spiritual source. However, you will be feel like a different person when you don't take your ego seriously.

I used to scoff at the question, "Who am I?" Now the question makes sense because I realize I am different when experiencing life through my heart than I am when experiencing life through my thought system and ego.

We create our ego subconsciously when we are very young and sense the need to prove ourselves or protect ourselves. It actually may have served us well at the time in dealing with people who were functioning from their own programmed thought system. Over time, the ego becomes more master than servant. While coming from our thought system, we fail to notice that this self-created ego is no longer useful or helpful. We find natural happiness when we recognize the ego for what it is and stop taking it seriously. Then we have access to the inner wisdom from our heart that truly serves us. We know we have nothing to prove. Instead we can enjoy *being*.

I can almost hear people object: "Isn't that selfish to sit around like a blob enjoying yourself?" *Being* who we truly are when we are no longer prisoners of our thought system does not mean we will sit around like selfish blobs. It means that what we do will be inspired from our heart. Our actions will not be contaminated or driven by past misperceptions that created the ego.

The fun thing about the ego is that every time we recognize it for what it is, we can't help laughing about it, thus causing it to lose its power. Our ego loves catching us off guard, however, so that it can sneak back. By keeping the principles in mind, you can play hide-and-seek with your ego.

Have you ever noticed how easy it is to observe illusionary ego beliefs in others, and how difficult it is to maintain that perspective with yourself? The thought systems and egos of characters in movies and novels become very obvious when observed through an *understanding* of the four principles. Life can be nicer when we have as much fun catching our own egos and observing our own thought system.

Like other illusions, insecurity loses its power once we know what it is. *Understanding* inspires love and compassion for ourselves, as well as for others who may not know their negative behavior is based on the illusions and insecurities of the thought system. The power of love from the heart is the only force that can overcome the effects of insecurity in the world.

JUDGMENTS

Many excuse their judgment of others by calling it "righteous" judgment. Righteous judgment is rare; because it is based on feelings of love and understanding, it leaves no negative feelings in its wake. Instead, the results of righteous judgment are positive. Abhorring child abuse is an example of righteous judgment when it is followed by actions to protect children and educate the parents out of love and compassion instead of self-righteousness.

"I'm telling you this for your own good" is not an example of righteous judgment, but of taking your own separate reality seriously and thinking it is the "right" reality. Self-righteous judgment of others is not helpful; it leaves negative feelings. When we dismiss our thought system, we rise to a higher level of consciousness where judgments are replaced with love, compassion, and inspiration about what to do.

Debra was having negative feelings about her friend Georgia, who was living her life in ways that "looked negative" to Debra. Debra decided to stay away from her for a while, which could have been a reasonable solution if Debra had simply stayed away without making judgments of Georgia or herself. Debra contaminated her decision, however, by judging herself. "If I were a bigger person, I wouldn't let her behavior bother me. I should be more loving and understanding." Debra's self-judgments kept her in a low mood, limited her perspective and produced more judgments of her friend.

She judged Georgia, too: "She is being so self-centered, self-righteous, manipulative, and self-serving. She thinks her reality is the only valid one in the world." Debra was able to find several others who had the same judgments about Georgia, which seemed to justify her own thoughts.

Debra's stomach was in knots as she continued the vicious cycle of self-condemnation and judgment of Georgia. Finally she used her feelings as a compass and could see her judgments for the thoughts they were. Debra decided to get quiet and look for the gift (or lesson) in this situation.

Being without judgment is being in a state of humility and quiet. During the "quiet," Debra's understanding deepened. She had a mirror insight: She *saw* that she often did all the same "selfish" things she attributed to Georgia. She saw that her judgments about Georgia were "self-centered, self-righteous, manipulative, and self-serving." It had been easier to see these "faults" in Georgia because they seemed worse than her own. From her inner wisdom, Debra realized that what she saw in Georgia was only a reflection of her own behavior, even though it wasn't "as bad."

Debra and Georgia are now great friends. Debra sees all Georgia's actions as endearing—or looks in the mirror at her own reflection if anything starts to bother her. These mirror insights help her *see* her own thought system at work. She can then laugh, drop the thoughts, and enjoy her natural good feelings.

STEREOTYPING

Another danger of judgment is that we often characterize people by what they do from their thought system, and decide this is the sum total of who they are. Often we dismiss what they do from their heart as "just an act." In so doing, we have taken the detour of believing in the reality of the thought system instead of the reality of the heart. We are more willing to trust the validity of behavior from a low mood than behavior from a high mood. This is mischievous behavior from the ego, trying to convince us that we are better if others seem worse.

JUDGMENTS FROM OTHERS

With *understanding,* we pay no more attention to the judgments of others than to our own. We see that we get into enough trouble taking our own judgments seriously, and that shoulds and shouldn'ts are no more helpful from others than they are from ourselves.

Virginia dreaded being around her mother for long because she felt intimidated by her mother's judgments, which she reacted to with rebellion. Her mother reacted to Virginia's rebellion with more judgments.

After learning about the principles, Virginia spent a delightful four days traveling across the country with her mother. As Virginia tells the story, "Every time my mom came out with what I used to call a judgment, I just saw it as her reality. Instead of rebelling and letting her know that I thought what she thought was stupid, I saw it as interesting. I could even see the insecurity behind her so-called judgments and feel compassion for her. I still didn't agree with her on everything, but I respected her right to see things differently. I was also able to respect my own way of seeing things, without getting huffy about it. We had a great time. We talked and shared more than we have in my whole life."

LIVING FOR—OR AGAINST—SOMEONE ELSE

Often we take the detour of trying to live up to the expectations of others and become "pleasers," or "approval junkies." By doing so, we discount our own inner wisdom and inspiration. Other times we take the detour of rebelling against the expectations of others, even when following their suggestions might be to our benefit. It is easy to understand why and how we create this part of our thought system when we look at our childhood conditioning about the need to live up to the expectations of parents and teachers. When we are little, the approval of others is very important to us. We form all kinds of beliefs about what we need to do to get approval, and how to protect ourselves when we don't.

Once there was a little girl named Marie who went to visit her aunt and uncle, where she learned how to make bread. Her aunt and uncle thought that was wonderful and praised her and told her over and over how much they appreciated her bread.

Marie went home and baked bread for her family. No one said anything about her bread, but just ate it. Marie decided she would never make bread for her family again because they didn't appreciate it and praise her.

Then one day she discovered she enjoyed making bread for the fun of it. She loved getting her hands into the dough to knead it; she loved the aroma of the baking bread; and she especially loved eating it hot out of the oven, dripping with butter and sometimes honey. She also loved sharing it with anyone who wanted to have some. She realized that when she was living for or against someone else, she didn't taste the bread.

SELF-ESTEEM

Self-esteem is one of the natural good feelings inherent in every human being when living from the heart. Self-esteem is a moment-to-moment state of mind. When we are listening to our inner wisdom, we have it, but when we are dependent on the approval of others or following false notions from the thought system, we don't. We have self-esteem when we esteem ourselves enough to listen to the messages from our heart.

An extremely popular detour is the one of "working on" self-esteem. Since lack of self-esteem is an illusion that exists only in the thought system, it makes no sense to give the illusion credibility by trying to *attain* self-esteem. Focusing on self-esteem is a detour guaranteed to lead you away from your natural, inherent self-esteem. As with happiness, we can't find self-esteem by looking for it. We have inherent and natural self-esteem and happiness when we dismiss the thought system that keeps them buried.

ANGER

It takes little to take us down the "big A" detour when our thought system is in control. We may get angry when people don't drive the way we want them to or when others don't respond as want them to, at exactly the moment we want them to (preferably by reading our mind). We may get angry when equipment doesn't work the way we want it to, or when a retail clerk doesn't behave as though we are the most important customer in the store. We get especially angry when someone else gets mad at us. I'm sure you could add to this list.

It is important to remember that all negative reactions are based on subconsciously stored thoughts and beliefs. As the *Course in Miracles* teaches in lesson 5, "I am never upset for the reason I think."[1] Lesson 7 teaches, "I see only the past."[2] This is an excellent description of the thought system. Everything we see from our thought system is seen through the filters of our past. When we do not *understand* these perception prisons, we are blocked from our ability to see with fresh perspective from our inner wisdom.

When we see our anger as reality, we have different ways of expressing it. Sometimes we verbalize anger, sometimes we sulk, and sometimes we have a silent tantrum against ourselves and get depressed. We miss so much of the beauty of life when we take this detour.

Another common detour is the belief that there are certain things that justify anger. It is normal to feel angry when we have been violated in any way. However, maintained anger over this or any other immoral act does not solve anything; it just makes us feel bad and keeps us from enjoying life *now*, or from accessing our inner wisdom to know what to do.

One therapist worked in group-therapy sessions with sixty women, victims of rape or incest. For many

---

[1] *A Course in Miracles: Workbook for Students* (Huntington Station, New York: The Foundation for Inner Peace), p. 8.
[2] Ibid., p. 11.

years these women talked about their anger, beat on pillows, and yelled and screamed about their anger. They spent hours confirming that what had happened to them in the past was the reason they could not hold jobs, were alcoholics, and could not participate in lasting relationships.

After the therapist learned about the four principles, she apologized to the women in her groups, "I'm sorry, ladies, but I have been doing it all wrong. From now on we will no longer dwell on the past, but will talk about some principles that will teach you how to have happiness and peace of mind in life now."

A few women dropped out because they did not want to give up their anger. The remaining women soon learned to enjoy life when they stopped living in the past through their thought system. A two-year follow-up showed they maintained their good feelings and were successful in their jobs and relationships. Some were training to become therapists or educators so they could share what they had learned.

One woman appeared on a panel with other rape victims. She was obviously a very happy person. The moderator of the panel questioned her, "Don't you feel angry? Hasn't your rape experience affected your relationship with men? Why are you so happy?"

"That experience took up eleven minutes of my life," she answered. "I don't intend to give it one more second in my thoughts. Life is so full of good things to enjoy, why should I waste time thinking about the past?"

When we don't like what happened in the past, it doesn't make sense to keep re-creating it in our thoughts and then multiplying the unhappiness by adding anger. Your anger has a message for you. Anger turns into resentment when you miss the message but keep the messenger. Try the methods of quieting discussed in chapter 9. Listen. Be gentle with yourself, and listen. Like all negative thoughts, anger loses its power when seen with *understanding*. From your heart, you will know what to do.

There is a popular opinion that if you don't get your anger out, you will store it, and it will fester. This can be true. Stored anger based on past stored perceptions can fester into physical disease; and it can destroy relationships. Biofeedback research suggests that one moment of thought-provoked anger substantially suppresses the immune system for eight hours. Other research demonstrates the healing effectiveness of the natural good feelings from the heart.

Obviously, it is not a good idea to store anger. The key is *how* to get it out. One way is to *understand* the thinking ability that created the thoughts that led to anger, and dismiss it. Another way is to share how you feel (not how someone else has "made" you feel) in a way that invites clarification of separate realities. What you do is not as important as the state of mind behind what you do. Sharing how you feel from your heart is very different from sharing your feelings from your thought system.

Another way to get anger out (literally) is to look for the lesson, or gift. We have already discussed how "looking in the mirror" for reflections of yourself can lead to *understanding* as you see the message or the life lesson. Seeing the message often leads to forgiveness.

Forgiveness transforms anger. Forgiveness is automatic when you see others or circumstances from your heart. The heart sees innocence. The heart feels compassion. The heart *understands*. You may need to get quiet for a while before you see through the eyes of your heart.

Sometimes it takes a healing process to expose the subconscious thought or belief behind anger, hurt, or any other debilitating emotion. An important part of healing is "walking in another person's shoes. . . . Go into that person's head to understand and identify their thoughts and feelings and intentions."[3] This helps one to truly understand separate realities and see with understanding, compassion, and forgiveness. Healing can be so complete that old beliefs and decisions from the past are gone.

THE PAST

Another popular detour is into the past. The past cannot exist unless we think about it, yet many live their whole lives on this detour.

Through brain research, it has been discovered that our brain is a storage container for everything in our past. Wilder Penfield found that he could probe any part of the brain and the patient would remember

[3]Valerie Seeman Moreton, N.D., *Heal the Cause* (San Diego: Kalos Publishing, 1996), p. 339.

135

the details of specific events from the past, including smells and feelings. "When Penfield and Jasper considered their results, it appeared that the brain held an untold number of film clips, each with sound and picture, of vivid events from the patient's past. The replaying would evoke, as well, the emotions that accompanied the original experiences."[4]

The brain also stores our interpretations of past events, even though they are not correct. The thought system turns these interpretations into beliefs that act as filters to keep us from seeing the truth in the moment.

For example, as children we may have decided we were unlovable or inadequate. This decision was not made based on the truth. Our parents may have reprimanded us out of love, or simply been too busy to give us the attention we wanted. The truth did not matter so much as our *interpretation* of the situation, which was cemented into a belief. This belief now may act as a filter to keep us from accepting love in the present. *Understanding* can eliminate the belief. When we *see* and interpret an event differently, from our heart, our feelings and decisions will also change.

Linda had an experience in her past in which it seemed to her that her father was embarrassed to hug her. She assumed he didn't love her, which she interpreted to mean she was not lovable. If she was not lovable to her own father, then she must not be lov-

[4]Jefferson Lewis, *Something Hidden: A Biography of Wilder Penfield* (Garden City, New York: Doubleday & Company, Inc., 1981), pp. 198–201

able to anyone. She constantly tried to prove she was worthy of love, but because her behavior was based on insecurity, she acted demanding and unlovable. She went to a therapist who tried to help her "get in touch with her anger at her father." In her heart, this did not feel right to Linda. Years later she found a therapist who taught her the four principles.

Understanding helped Linda dismiss her thought system. Inspiration from her heart helped her see that her father felt uncomfortable hugging not because he didn't love her, but because he had never received affection himself. She had another healing insight: She knew that even if her father had *not* loved her, that would have been a consequence of his thought system, not an indication that she was unworthy of being loved.

When we understand that the past exists only when we think about it and that it is only our interpretation of what happened, it becomes difficult to take our thoughts about the past seriously. In the same way, when we see the innocence of others' past actions, knowing they did the best they could from their level of understanding at the time, we will feel differently about those actions.

Paula often complained about all the terrible things her mother had done and said to her in the past. A therapist asked her, "Do you think your mother stayed up late at night plotting ways to make your life miserable?"

With reluctance, Paula admitted, "No."

A week later Paula said that that question had helped her understand the principle of separate realities, and led her out of her thought system to her heart where she felt compassion and forgiveness. It had become clear to her that her mother really did love her, and had done the best she could, considering her own insecurities.

Paula added that her inner wisdom then led her to "look in the mirror" and see how she was repeating many of the same behaviors with her own son. "I punish him when he makes mistakes, even though I hated it when my mother did that. I can see now that she probably did it for the same reasons I do. I'm afraid that if I don't punish him he won't learn to do better, and I want him to do better because I love him. But when I was a child I can remember wishing my mother would understand how I felt and teach me with love instead of punishment."

Paula was able to forgive her mother and herself when she understood that the "mistakes" they had both made were simply the results of getting sidetracked from love and enjoyment of their children into thoughts that produced fear and insecurity.

LIGHTEN UP, KEEP IT SIMPLE, AND COME FROM LOVE

When I am miserably on my way down the path of low moods, I have usually taken three detours at once. I have taken my perceptions seriously (usually having to do with ego, expectations, and judgments). I have then tried to analyze complicated ways to solve the problem. And third, I am coming from perceptions of insecurity that manifest themselves in anger or hopelessness. In other words, from this state of mind all the possible, complicated solutions don't really seem like solutions at all, but more like ways of seeking revenge or escape. What detours! As soon as I tune into my inner wisdom (sometimes in minutes, sometimes in days) I can see what I have done and feel inspired to lighten up, keep it simple, and come from love.

Lightening up usually involves raising your perspective so you see the big picture. When you lighten up and quit taking things too seriously, what once seemed like a tragedy can now be seen as an interesting event, as a stepping-stone rather than a stumbling block, as a great gift full of lessons to be learned, or perhaps simply a humorous situation.

Keeping it simple usually means that the solution becomes obvious and uncomplicated when we drop the anger, hatred, and revenge. Trying to figure things out from our thought system is usually complicated; figuring things out from our heart (love) is simple.

Coming from love means that what you do is not as important as how you do it. For example, maybe it would be a wise thing to ground your child, or fire an employee, or leave a relationship. This can be done with love and respect rather than with anger and revenge. When you are doing the obvious thing to handle a situation, there is no need for anger. Lighten up, keep it simple, and come from love.

IT GETS EASIER TO AVOID DETOURS

Even a limited understanding of the principles keeps us pointed in the right direction so that our understanding keeps getting deeper. The deeper the understanding, the easier it gets.

Let good feelings from your heart be your only guide to avoid detours, to enjoy the detours, or to find your way back home.

12

Relationships

The four principles can show us where problems in a relationship originate:

1. Trying to change someone else's reality—fighting over who is right instead of respecting differences and finding them interesting.

2. Getting caught up in negative thoughts—judgments, interpretations, the past, proving ego and self-importance, and other forms of thought-produced insecurity—which happens when we focus on the content of our thoughts instead of realizing that thinking is a function.

3. Not dismissing negative thoughts (or at least not getting quiet) during low moods or low levels of consciousness, but instead trying to discuss them, figure them out, or solve them.

4. Sharing negative feelings that come from the insecurity of our thought systems, with the

belief that our partners should understand them, take them seriously, and adopt them as their own reality, instead of using our feelings compass to let us know where we are.

When we don't understand these principles, we often react from the fears and old beliefs of our thought system instead of acting from the love of our heart and inner wisdom.

SEPARATE REALITIES RELATING TO RELATIONSHIPS

Amy and Sean had daily arguments. No matter what the subject, the theme was always the same.

Amy: "You have to be blind as a bat not to see things my way!"

Sean: "If you had any brains at all, you would know that *my* way is right!"

Amy and Sean are both stuck in the illusions of their separate realities.

Have you ever tried to convince your partner that your point of view was the right one, and felt as if you were talking to a wall? You were actually talking to two walls—the wall of your own unique reality and the wall of your partner's unique reality. (Literally talking to a wall could be easier because a wall does not have its own point of view, and you wouldn't have any expectations from a wall.) It is even less productive to try convincing your partner, who already knows how things are and would like to convince you. Your partner is usually seeing his or her reality with as much inner wisdom as you are seeing yours: zero.

Jeannette strongly believed her children needed lots of rules and guidance; Duane believed he should sacrifice anything important to him in order to cater to their whims. Duane thought Jeannette was a tyrant; Jeannette thought Duane was a wimp. Both were so entrenched in their separate realities that they could not access their inner wisdom. Sometimes wisdom might take the form of guidance, sometimes the form of doing things with or for others. In either case, guidance or doing things for others based on good feelings and inspiration from their hearts will be different from those actions based on self-righteousness, defensiveness, or judgment from their thought systems.

When we take our reality seriously, it becomes an interesting frame of reference—or a distorted pair of glasses. We don't realize how those glasses distort and filter everything in our world. When we dismiss our judgments and expectations, we see a very different and interesting person in front of us.

Dorene and Charles were experiencing marital difficulty because they were deeply enmeshed in their separate realities. Their distorted frames of reference prevented them from seeing anything with love and compassion.

Dorene complained about being third or fourth priority in Charles' life. From this belief, she felt hurt. As many of us do, she covered her hurt feelings with anger, which she expressed by blaming and attacking Charles for not putting her first.

Charles took her attacks seriously and generated feelings of inadequacy and defensiveness, which he expressed by acting disdainful toward Dorene. Charles' frame of reference included a belief that women were unfair and unreasonable anyway.

During her childhood, Dorene had had an experience that she had interpreted to mean that she was unimportant. She turned this interpretation into a belief that distorted every experience she had from then on. Subconsciously, she spent her life looking for evidence to support her belief in her unimportance, and she was so intent on this task that she missed any evidence that might change her belief.

This was obvious when she told the story of how she and Charles met and got married. Charles was dating Adele, but quit seeing her and soon asked Dorene to marry him. Dorene did not see this as evidence that she was important to Charles. What she did notice was Adele's name on the wedding invitation list, which she saw as evidence that Adele was more important to him than she was. Charles' attempts to explain that he simply liked Adele as a friend fell on deaf ears.

Charles, in turn, had once had a childhood experience that he had interpreted to mean that women were unfair and unreasonable. He adopted this as such a strong belief that he was unaware of how he set women up to prove he was right. In this case, he knew Dorene would probably be upset if he put Adele's name on the list, but, although it wasn't important to have Adele as a wedding guest, he wanted to be able to prove he was right about how unreasonable women can be. Of course, he claimed it was important because he had to justify his position.

You and I have enough perspective (because we are removed) to see the humor in the emotions and dramas they created by their thinking, but Dorene and Charles were not laughing. When we take the filters from our thought system seriously, it is impossible to see the situation with perspective.

Dorene and Charles were focused on what they were looking for through the filters of their thought systems, which left little time to share good feelings. When our attention is focused on looking for evidence to support our distorted beliefs, we miss the obvious, wonderful things going on around us.

We can always create what we are looking for. For instance, if we believe we will be rejected, we will act in such a way that invites rejection, or we will see rejection even in innocent behaviors.

After hearing about the four principles, Dorene and Charles finally dismissed their thoughts and saw each other very differently. They stopped "playing detective," looking for evidence to support their insecurities, and started seeing things from their hearts instead of their heads. Charles felt like reassuring Dorene that she was important, and Dorene felt like reassuring Charles that she trusted him. Neither one really needed reassurance anymore, but each appreciated the loving gestures. They had learned to laugh at their silly thoughts and see the beauty of life and of each other.

ACCEPTANCE

A marriage counselor suggested to Hazel that she stop trying to change her husband and accept him the way he was. Three months later Hazel complained, "But I *have* accepted him for three whole months, and he hasn't changed a bit!" Would you say Hazel's idea of acceptance was conditional?

Acceptance is *understanding* that everyone has a separate reality. Acceptance means respecting differences, not conditional acceptance while expecting changes. Even though it is impossible to change other people's realities (only they can do that by changing their own thoughts), we often keep trying. True acceptance is unconditional and allows us to see others with compassion, gratitude, and love.

THOUGHTS AND MOODS RELATING TO RELATIONSHIPS

Mary thought Jim was not paying enough attention to her. When she self-righteously shared this with her friends, they told her the importance of letting him know how she felt. Mary decided that was a good idea, so that night when Jim sat down on the couch and started to read the newspaper, she sat next to him and said, "How come the newspaper is more important to you than I am?"

Jim defensively retorted, "Because the newspaper doesn't hassle me."

Mary ran to the bedroom and cried, and for the rest of the evening she did not speak to Jim. The next day she told all her friends that Jim had admitted he preferred the newspaper to her, so she might as well get a divorce.

Fortunately Mary had an opportunity to learn about the principles. She dismissed the notions of insecurity from her thought system and was amazed how much her feelings about herself and Jim changed when she saw the world from her heart.

The next time Jim sat down to read the newspaper, she sat quietly next to him, feeling gratitude for having such a nice man for a husband. She could see past his defensive behavior and felt unconditional love because she had dismissed her own insecurities, judgments, and expectations.

Soon Jim put down the newspaper and gruffly asked, "Did you want to talk?"

Mary could feel that he was still in a low mood and replied, "No, I was just enjoying your presence." Suspiciously, Jim continued to read the newspaper. For several weeks Mary continued to enjoy just being with Jim, no matter what he did. She had discovered her own inner happiness and peace of mind and was not affected by outside circumstances.

One day Jim came into the kitchen while Mary was preparing dinner. She asked, "Did you want something?"

"No," he replied, "I just wanted to be with you."

Some people who hear this story think Mary acted like a wimp who decided to passively put up with a jerk. But look at her results: She found serenity, saw the goodness beneath Jim's gruffness, and inspired him to experience his own heart. Unconditional love has the power to lead others to their heart center.

Another person might follow his or her wisdom to do something else. When living in the heart there are infinite possibilities about what to do, but the feelings behind the doing will be the same—compassion, forgiveness, gratitude, and all the other feelings that are the essence of love.

We create our world from our thoughts and actions. We reap what we sow: When we put negativity out into the world, we get negativity back. Yet when negativity comes back, most people forget they put it out in the first place; they don't take responsibility for its creation by their thoughts and subsequent actions. (Mary did not see that she helped create Jim's defensiveness and gruffness with her expectations and criticism.) In the same way, when we put love out into the world, love comes back. Joy and happiness are contagious.

Are you still arguing that sometimes negative circumstances come to you even when you did nothing to create them? The point is that even if you have no personal responsibility for causing certain events, your *thoughts about them* give you more trouble than the circumstances themselves.

Sue's husband had an affair, and she was so hurt that she wanted revenge. She went to an attorney and said, "I want to hurt him as much as he hurt me. I want to leave him with as little as possible financially, and to limit his child visitation rights as much as possible. I will make sure the kids don't even want to see him."

Sue was too hurt and angry to see that it was her thoughts about this situation that made her miserable. Fortunately she chose a wise attorney, who asked, "Do you really want to hurt him in the worst way possible?"

"Yes."

The attorney said, "Then go back and live with him for six months. Be the very best wife you can imagine: Be loving, compassionate, understanding, forgiving, affectionate, and fun to be with. He will feel lucky and will start loving you very much. In six months you can start divorce proceedings, which will hurt him emotionally and financially."

Sue objected, "I couldn't stand to live with him for six more months."

"Well, then you must not really want to hurt him in the worst way possible."

"Oh, yes I do," Sue said. "I will do it."

Two years later the attorney saw Sue walking down a street. He asked, "What happened? I thought you were going to come back for a divorce."

Sue replied, "Are you kidding? He is the most wonderful man in the world. I wouldn't even think of leaving him." She must have done such a good job acting loving that she soon forgot it was an act and started enjoying the good feelings. Good feelings are extremely contagious, creating more good feelings in people who come in contact with them.

When *understanding* changes how we see things, everything and everyone in our world looks different. It may seem as though others have changed, but it is our thoughts, and thus our reality, and thus our feelings that have changed. Others often respond to our feeling level. When we give love, we get love—not necessarily because others give it back to us, but because love will emanate from within. Feeling love does not depend on anything or anyone else.

You may ask, "But what if I just don't feel loving, and I'm not willing to 'act' as Sue did?" Whenever we feel the need to ask what to do, it is helpful to do nothing except dismiss our thoughts, get quiet, and wait until we feel good enough to know from our inner wisdom what to do.

And if you don't feel ready, you don't feel ready. What is, is. To simply accept *what is* can be very calming.

Remember that sometimes awareness of the principles will change our mood instantly, and we will tap into our heart and inner wisdom. Other times we may see that focusing on the content of our thoughts is producing our negative feelings, but we won't feel better immediately. Those times are more like when we have the flu; we have a level of understanding that doesn't change our state of mind immediately, but it may lead us to quietly take care of ourselves until our mood passes.

I realized this after an experience of being caught up in thinking my reality was much better than my husband's. I really believed he was wrong, and since it seemed so real to me, I certainly had to tell him about it. (Have you ever noticed that when you think other people are "wrong," you feel compelled to inform them?)

My tirade lasted about five minutes before my miserable feelings alerted me to what I was doing. Although I immediately shut up, I still didn't feel much better; I simply saw enough to get quiet and quit spreading my negative emotions around. I started thinking, "I should apologize." But I didn't feel like apologizing, so I just stayed quiet.

I forget how long it took me to feel better, because I stopped thinking about my negative emotions, but the next day when I was feeling love and gratitude for my husband, we talked about what had happened. Since I was then in a loving mood, it felt natural to apologize without feeling blame and guilt. Barry said that he was aware my silence the day before was different from my old sulky silences that sent out vibrations of anger and blame. He said, "It was very nice."

Another time I became upset when my husband and I missed an opportunity to go on a trip with friends because he had a hunting trip planned. I had several negative thoughts that gave me some bad feelings. I knew I was caught up in my thought system, but I didn't get quiet. Instead, I asked Barry, "Would you like to hear my crazy thoughts?"

Barry replied good-humoredly, "Sure. Go ahead."

I said, "Hunting is more important to you than I am."

Barry calmly replied, "You know that isn't true. I had this planned way ahead. I'll be more than happy to take a trip with you anytime we can find a mutually agreeable time."

I humorously admitted, "I know, but I used to get away with it."

In the past I believed my silly thoughts about hunting being more important to Barry than I was. The important difference this time was that I accepted responsibility for my crazy thinking. Even though I felt disappointed, I couldn't take it as seriously as I did when I didn't know I was thinking from my thought system—and so this time I couldn't use it for manipulative purposes.

My awareness of "doing my insecurity number" made it impossible for those feelings to have much power. It was not long before I could see that I didn't need a trip to be happy. I didn't even need to be more important than hunting to be happy.

Intellectual understanding does not change our feelings, but it can help us dismiss our thoughts, or at least take them less seriously, until we receive inspiration from our heart.

LISTENING

True listening is forgetting about the details, hearing what another person is feeling, and knowing when those feelings are coming from thoughts of insecurity. We recognize the difference from our own feeling level. When we feel love, compassion, or interest rather than judgment or defensiveness, we are listening deeply. *Understanding* changes the experience of listening.

When your partner is upset or caught up in thought, that is the time to listen, not to talk. Analyzing does not help. Listening is quietly responding with love. When we are in that state of mind, our inspiration will let us know exactly how to express love and encouragement—eventually, if not immediately. It might be humor. It might be time alone. It might be a loving touch. It might be a quiet walk. It might be time to rest. It might be time for reflective listening. We will know.

Another way for couples to avoid low moods, is to avoid the thought system by just having fun together.

HAVE FUN TOGETHER

Have you ever noticed that when you are having fun together you are not being judgmental, critical, or dissatisfied? Having fun can act as a catalyst to take us out of our thought system. When we want to experience love and good feelings in our relationships, it makes sense to do things together that bring pleasure and enjoyment.

LIVE IN GRATITUDE

When we dismiss negative thoughts, we are left with feelings of gratitude and appreciation for all that life has to offer. It makes no sense to live in negativity when love is just a dropped thought away. When following the treasure map to happiness and peace of mind, the natural state of a relationship is to enjoy unconditional love.

13

Myths about Relationships

As the following myths are presented, reality as seen through our heart and inner wisdom is shown to be the opposite of what many of us have been taught all our lives.

MYTH NO. 1: LOVE IS BLIND

Love is not blind. When we are in love, we are not blinded by judgments, expectations, and other kinds of filters from our thought system. We see differences as interesting, or with understanding and compassion. What other people might see as faults in our beloved, we find endearing, we defend against, or we brush off as unimportant.[1]

Because Bob promised to call Nancy at 9:30, but didn't call until 11:00, she thought he was inconsiderate and uncaring—and told him so. Her feelings let her know she was in her thought system. This *understanding* immediately took her to her heart and she remembered that when they had fallen in love, she had been understanding and compassionate when he called later than promised. It became obvious to her that it wasn't the circumstances but her thoughts that upset her. Her judgments and anger were her defense mechanisms to cover up feelings of insecurity. From her heart, she felt secure and loving again.

When we look through our judgment glasses, we see differences or circumstances without love or compassion. The judgment blinder is so powerful that it can even change what was once seen as a virtue into a "fault."

Marilyn fell in love with Jordan and admired the calm way he drove a car, which made her feel safe and relaxed on rides with him. After they got married, however, she found it often drove her crazy to ride with him because he was not aggressive enough and didn't take risks to pass slow cars.

Marilyn had also admired Jordan for his quiet, easygoing dependability; he had been in the same

---

[1]It is important to note that these attitudes also could come from the thought system based on seeing a person through filters of who we think they are rather than who they are. When this is true, we become disappointed when they don't live up to our expectations. When coming from our heart, disappointment never follows.

job for twelve years, and she could set her clock by his departure and arrival. With her judgment glasses on, however, she started seeing him as boring and lacking in ambition. During their courtship, she had loved his flexibility and willingness to go along with all her suggestions. But through her judgment blinders she saw him as spineless and weak, without an original thought in his head.

Marilyn divorced Jordan and married Steve, who was aggressive, ambitious, and opinionated. At first Marilyn admired these "virtues" in Steve and felt lucky to be married to an exciting man who knew what he wanted and where he was going. She felt protected and taken care of. Later, however, she saw him as controlling and unyielding because he would not do what she wanted him to do, and instead of feeling protected, she felt dominated and not taken seriously.

Marilyn divorced Steve and married another man like Jordan. She is now in her seventh marriage because she does not see that she loses her good feelings and happiness every time she puts on her blinders of judgment and expectation. She believes she sees reality through her blinders. She is also looking for happiness outside herself and blames others when she doesn't find it there.

From her heart, Marilyn would not need to look for love outside herself. She would be loving.

This may sound very idealistic and altruistic, but it is natural from our heart. It becomes idealistic and altruistic only when we think we *should* be loving from our thought system.

157

MYTH NO. 2: IT IS IMPORTANT TO BE COMPATIBLE

Dolores divorced Scott. Her explanation: "We just weren't compatible." A pervasive distortion of the meaning of compatibility is the notion that two people must have the same beliefs and interests to live together harmoniously.

When we understand the principle of separate realities, we can see that it is impossible for two people to be the same. Couples fooled into thinking they have the same interests and beliefs get into trouble when they later find what they thought was the same is not.

Dolores and Scott were delighted to discover they both enjoyed tennis. They were already in love, but saw their mutual interest in tennis as proof they were "compatible." The trouble started because Dolores liked to play more often than Scott did, and he thought she took it too seriously. Dolores assumed that anyone really interested in tennis would feel exactly the same way she did about it. They both felt cheated and misunderstood, and, since they were apparently not as compatible as they had thought, divorce was the only solution they could see.

The true meaning of compatibility is having the ability to live together in harmony. We all have this ability because compatibility is a natural state when we dismiss negative thoughts and respect differences instead of judging them.

Lillian was feeling dissatisfied with Garth because she claimed they had nothing in common. She felt they would both be better off if they broke off their relationship and went their separate ways. Garth felt very hurt and lashed out, "You couldn't have a long-lasting relationship with anyone!"

Lillian replied indignantly, "How could you say such a stupid thing? I have had friends for years all over the country, even though we don't see each other often. And they are all deep friendships."

The next day Lillian saw a therapist who taught her about the four principles. Lillian felt good when she left the therapist's office, but a few hours later started thinking again about what Garth has said. She felt the anger well up again. She decided to take the therapist's advice to get quiet and look for the message in the anger. It did not take long for her to receive an insight that made her laugh. She realized that she treated her friends with unconditional love and respect. She never criticized or judged or burdened them with her expectations. When they were down, she encouraged them; when they were up, she celebrated with them. Her love relationships started out the same way, but she would soon move away from her heart and into her head.

As soon as she realized this, she was able to laugh at herself, drop her insecure thoughts, and start treating Garth the way she did her friends. Their love blossomed.

It is unimportant to be compatible in today's commonly (and narrowly) defined way; we don't need to have the same interests and beliefs. We have compatibility when we see differences with interest, respect, and love. We are compatible when we share good feelings rather than judgments and expectations.

We are naturally compatible when we experience life through our heart and inner wisdom rather than through our thought system.

MYTH NO. 3: IT IS IMPORTANT TO COMMUNICATE ABOUT PROBLEMS

An overemphasis on the importance of communication in relationships is another pervasive distortion. How often have you heard someone say, "We just can't communicate," or, "The key to a good relationship is communication"?

The distortion in these statements is the implied importance of making your partner understand and accept what you feel and what you believe. That is, if you can get your partner to believe your reality rather than his or her own, you have succeeded in "good" communication. This is the same as saying, "You should have my illusions, not your own."

No wonder almost everyone is failing in their attempts at communication. It is impossible for your partner to believe your reality rather than his or her own. With *understanding,* you both might dismiss your realities for the illusions of thought that they are, but until then you would "rather fight than switch."

Because we are always communicating, either from our distorted thought system (fear) or from our heart (love), it is important to know where our communication is coming from. When we are communicating from our thought system, we are sharing negative feelings, thoughts, and beliefs. Even sulky or angry silences are a form of communication. When we are communicating from our heart, however, we are sharing the positive feelings we experience through love, wisdom, and inspiration.

Sharing positive feelings is often done silently. Many couples do more quiet touching and less verbal communication when they realize how inadequate words are to express beautiful feelings. When we are in a state of happiness and peace of mind, it is amazing how much we can enjoy what is usually referred to as mundane information. "Is dinner ready?" "I paid the bills today." "How are the kids?" "Shall we go to the beach?" Communication becomes light and easy, not heavy as it is when we communicate to "get it all out" or to make sure our partner knows how we feel (from our thought system).

This may sound boring to some people, but happiness and peace of mind are not boring. In that state of mind, it is common to feel so full of the joy of living and love for our partners that we are filled with gratitude.

You may be wondering, "Does this mean we shouldn't talk about our separate realities?" What we do is not the point. Talking about our separate realities, or not talking about them, is simply a different experience when we understand the principles. It is not what we *do* that is important, but the feeling behind what we do. With *understanding,* you will probably feel a sense of humor if you do talk about separate realties, instead of taking them seriously.

MYTH NO. 4: NEVER GO TO SLEEP UNTIL YOU HAVE RESOLVED AN ARGUMENT

Sometimes the best way to dismiss thoughts of right and wrong is to set some kind of cooling-off period to help us get quiet. This could be done by sleeping it off, walking around the block, or doing something else that helps us feel better.

Kate and Frank believed they should never go to sleep until they had resolved their arguments. They would stand toe to toe and argue about who was right and who was wrong. Since they were both caught up in their individual thought systems and separate realities, it was impossible to hear each other or solve anything. Since they believed they should be able to solve their arguments, their frustrations would build. Frank would finally leave, slamming the door behind him, and go to the nearest bar. Kate would go to bed, but couldn't sleep because she was furiously thinking about their failure to solve the problem before going to sleep.

When they saw a therapist who taught them about the principles, they saw what they could do. Frank said to Kate, "Since I like to leave the house when I am upset, I will leave, but I won't slam the door, and I won't go to a bar. I'll take a walk around the block until my thought system is tucked away where it can't hurt me, and I am able to enjoy how much I love you again. You can know that my leaving is not anger at you, but just my recognition that I'm caught up in my negative thoughts and need to get quiet until they go away."

Kate said, "Since I enjoy relaxing in bed, I will do that. But instead of continuing to think about my negative thoughts, I will read a book or go to sleep with the reassuring knowledge that they are just thoughts. You can know I'm not going to bed to get away from you, but to rest until the negative thoughts are gone and nothing is left but love."

MYTH NO. 5: A RELATIONSHIP WITHOUT FIGHTS IS SUPERFICIAL OR ONE-SIDED

Couples who understand the principles do not fight, or at least they realize they are off track when they do. The peace between them does not mean that they are not going "deep enough" in their relationship or that one of them is surrendering too much. On the contrary, they respect each other instead of their programmed thought systems.

Sylvia said, "I can't remember the last time Tim and I had a fight. It has been at least four years. We had lots of fights before, but now we just enjoy each other."

"Lisa and I still have fights," said Scott, "but they are all silent. We know that if we feel like fighting we are just in a low mood, or lost in our thought systems, so we keep quiet and wait for it to pass."

Beth said, "Tom and I used to have fights and lose respect for each other. We still have fights once in a while, but now we lose respect for the fights instead of for each other."

"When Dave and I have fights now," said Kathie, "we seldom take them seriously for long, so we end up laughing. It is especially fun to watch my 'Sarah

163

Bernhardt act' while I am still taking things a little bit seriously."

I used to get upset when I wanted to "discuss" something with my husband, and he would tell me, "Forget it." I would retort, "What do you mean, 'Forget it'? If you had any sensitivity at all, you would be upset, too." Now I say, "Thanks for reminding me."

MYTH NO. 6: WE'LL BE HAPPY ONCE CIRCUMSTANCES CHANGE

Happiness is a state of mind that has nothing to do with circumstances. "Dear Abby" received a letter from a woman complaining about her husband's snoring. In reply, "Dear Abby" quoted a letter from another woman: "I used to complain about snoring. My husband is dead now. I would give anything to be able to hear him snoring again."

An often-told story is the one about struggling newlyweds who do not appreciate the joy of being to-gether and in love because they keep focusing on how much better it will be when they have more money, a house, and furniture. Then they get the money, house, and furniture, but don't enjoy them because they think they are not as much in love as they used to be. In fact they do not experience the joy of love because they keep focusing on circumstances. They cannot see what *is* when focusing on what *is not*. In our thought system, we want more, better, different. In our heart, we feel contentment and gratitude.

We experience joy in our relationships when we are loving unconditionally—when we take off our blinders and see our partner the same way we did when we fell in love. You might object, "But my wife is not the same as when we fell in love. She wasn't fat then." The answer to every possible objection can be found in the principles. Your happiness has nothing to do with what anyone else is or does. If you are seeing the fat, you are not seeing the insecurity, which you may have helped create. When you see with *love* instead of with *judgment*, you will also see solutions.

June was miserable because her husband, Cy, was an alcoholic. She vowed to herself that if he did not stop drinking by the time the children left home, she would leave him. They had been married thirty years when the last child left for college. Before June kept her vow, she decided to see a therapist, who taught her the principles. She decided to try meditation to see if could receive a message about what to do. She was surprised at the clear inspiration she received from her inner wisdom: "It is not your province to judge your husband, but to love him unconditionally." June's reality changed; she loved Cy unconditionally without effort, and within three months he stopped drinking.

Some people have interpreted this story to mean that a woman should deny the problems of alcoholism and become an "enabler" by ignoring the issue. If you have heard the principles with *understanding*, you realize that the story does not set forth a rule; it simply tells what happened to one woman who listened to the inspiration from her inner wisdom. Someone else might hear a totally different message. The message could be to leave with love or to lovingly insist on an intervention program. The possibilities are limitless. Only one thing will always be the same—positive results are experienced when we follow our inner wisdom.

MYTH NO. 7: JEALOUSY IS A SIGN OF CARING

Jealousy is created from the ego and is based on the notion that possessiveness will cure feelings of inadequacy. It is a way of trying to get someone else to take responsibility for our own happiness.

Jealousy is just insecurity produced by thoughts about ego and self-importance, which is based on an illusion of being unimportant. These insecurities usually take the form of a fear of inadequacy, fear of rejection, or a fear of powerlessness. Many people base their lives on these illusions, wasting time and energy trying to hide their fears, or trying to blame themselves or others as the cause of their fears.

Fears of inadequacy take such forms as, "I won't be good enough. Someone else will be better than I am. If only I were more beautiful (or handsome, powerful, successful, intelligent, witty), then I would be okay."

Fears of rejection take such forms as, "He won't care as much as I care, which means I'm not good enough, so he might leave me, and then I'll be alone and will never find anyone else."

Fears of powerlessness take such forms as, "I can't do anything about this. I have no control over what is happening to me. I can't make someone love me."

166

All these fears are self-worth issues. The belief that anyone can lack self-worth is an illusion based on years of conditioning from childhood. When we *understand* this, we can have compassion for ourselves for buying into the illusion, and compassion for those who perpetuated it out of their lack of *understanding*. Before *understanding*, however, the illusions created by the thought system are powerful detours away from happiness in relationships.

Bill and Sue went to a party. When he saw her dancing with another man he became angry. He sulked on the way home until Sue persuaded him to admit something was wrong. Then he blew! He blamed her for flirting and accused her of being inconsiderate. He would not accept her explanation that she didn't especially want to dance with the other man, but didn't know how to refuse gracefully.

Bill had become so lost in the contents of his thinking that he didn't connect his behavior with his original thoughts of insecurity. He had used blame to cover up his fear that Sue might find him inadequate compared to the other man and that she might decide to reject him—a fear against which he felt powerless. Expressing anger gave him a false sense of power and control—but certainly not happiness.

Bill decided to leave Sue, to protect himself from being left by her. He created the very thing he feared in order to protect himself from what he feared.

It is easy for us to see the absurdity when observing the illusions of others. Understanding helps us see the absurdity of our own illusions—with compassion.

MYTH NO. 8: YOU MUST HAVE A RELATIONSHIP

Who says you have to have a relationship?

This is just another belief based on another thought, and when you look at the evidence, it makes no sense. There are just as many (or more) *un*happy people in relationships as there are happy people in relationships. In fact, there are just as many who are happy even though they *don't* have a relationship as there are people unhappy because they don't have a relationship.

Again, it's not the circumstances themselves, but how you think about them. When we have peace of mind, gratitude, and satisfaction with all that *is*, we don't see what is not. We are happy with or without a relationship.

We can be in love with life, alone as well as with someone.

14

Wisdom—and Lack
of Wisdom—from the Ages

Wisdom from the ages makes sense at a deeper level
when we understand the principles of thinking as a
function, separate realities, levels of consciousness,
and feelings as a compass.

IF YOU CAN'T SAY SOMETHING
NICE, DON'T SAY ANYTHING AT ALL

Understanding that our reality is a creation of our
thoughts, rather than the only reality, it is easy to see
the wisdom in keeping silent when we have nothing
nice to say. It makes no sense to say something nasty
or judgmental about other realities. Since negative
feelings are simply an indicator of a low mood created
by our programmed thought system, it is wise not to
say anything at all during that time.

As soon as we dismiss our thought system, seeing or saying something unkind will not be part of our reality. From our heart, we see through the eyes of love and compassion. We know that other people are doing the best they can while seeing the world through the filters of their programmed thought system.

COUNT TO TEN

Counting to ten is a way of dismissing thought and getting quiet until low moods pass. Some of us may need to count to ten thousand. Looking for life lessons and mirror insight messages can be as effective as counting to ten. When nothing seems to work to pry us loose from our negative thoughts and feelings, we may need help to heal deeply programmed thoughts and beliefs.

TIME HEALS ALL WOUNDS

This is true only when that time is spent in quiet, or at least not thinking about whatever may have caused an emotional wound. Have you ever looked back and felt foolish about getting upset about something that now appears ridiculous and unimportant? This growth in perspective could be called "growing up," which happens naturally with time.

The thought system can stunt our growth and keep wounds from healing naturally. When we see the world through the filters of our thought system, we remain stuck in the past instead of experiencing life freshly, moment to moment. Rehashing old wounds is like pouring bacteria in a physical wound—the infection can be worse than the original trauma and can rob time of its power to heal.

Even though the body is designed to heal itself, some physical wounds take longer to heal than others. Likewise, some emotional wounds may take more time to heal than others. *Understanding* does not mean you will never feel hurt, sad, or angry. We would not be normal if we didn't feel sad over the loss of a loved one, angry at man's inhumanity to man, and hurt when our desires aren't fulfilled. However, even these events feel different from our heart where we can feel sadness over our loss, followed by gratitude for the time we had with our loved one; hurt, followed by gratitude for the life lessons we have learned; and anger, followed by compassion, forgiveness, and inner guidance about what to do when something needs to be done. This will include compassion for ourselves to take whatever time we need.

HASTE MAKES WASTE

The need to hurry to figure things out keeps us bogged down in our thought system. We gain perspective when we slow down and leave room for inspiration. From our heart or spiritual source, we usually find solutions in less time and with no effort. Stop thinking about it (whatever it is), slow down, enjoy life, and watch inspiration flow.

STICKS AND STONES MAY BREAK MY
BONES, BUT NAMES WILL NEVER HURT ME

Shari said, "I feel like a failure because my husband tells me I never do anything right. No wonder I don't have any self-esteem."

Shari's sense of failure comes not from her husband's criticisms, but from *her thoughts about* them. If Shari would dismiss her thoughts about her husband's comments, from her heart she would know that what he says comes from his separate reality. She would see the innocence and insecurity behind what he is saying.

With *understanding*, Shari would know what to do. Instead of taking his thoughts seriously, she might then feel inspired to hug him, make a joke, take a walk, or whatever her inner wisdom would lead her to do. Have you ever noticed that people tend not to use intimidation with people who don't get hooked by it? When Shari stops getting hooked, her husband might stop. If he doesn't, her inner wisdom can lead her to the next step.

A STITCH IN TIME SAVES NINE

The only stitch we need to take is to *understand* thought, and the trouble this will save us is greater than nine.

A small tear in a piece of cloth gets larger and larger unless it is stitched while it is still small. In the same way, a negative thought can grow more and more powerful unless it is dismissed as soon as you realize it is just a thought.

But there is also an interesting difference: When you let a tear in cloth get larger, it takes more work to fix it. Understanding makes it simple to dismiss the thought system. As soon as you recognize a thought for what it is, the negative power is gone. Inspiration from the heart is never work, but pleasure.

When you have an intellectual understanding of the principles, have tried getting quiet to wait for them to pass, but still feel stuck in negative thoughts and emotions, don't beat up on yourself. Everything is as it should be. Knowing this will keep you open to messages from your inner wisdom. It is not a coincidence that we find exactly what we need when we are open to guidance from our heart or spiritual source.

An understanding of the principles gives new meaning to many old sayings, but our understanding can also help us see the lack of wisdom in some of the old adages.

IDLENESS IS THE DEVIL'S WORKSHOP

Idleness is not a sin; it leaves room for inspiration. Nevertheless, so many people fear that if they are not constantly busy they will not be productive.

What is productivity? Productivity from inspiration produces happiness; productivity from the thought system produces unhappiness. We may be productive in achievement, material prosperity, or a spotless house, while our family life is falling apart. Or we may be productive trying to find satisfaction outside ourselves and wonder why we never feel satisfied.

Wayne Dyer tells a wonderful story in his tape series, "Secrets of the Universe."[1] Once there were two alley cats. The young cat spent his days frantically chasing his tail. One day the old alley cat wandered by and stopped to watch the young cat. He finally interrupted and asked, "Would you mind telling me what you are doing?"

The young alley cat stopped, took a few minutes to catch his breath, and explained, "I went to cat philosophy school and learned that happiness is in the end of our tails. I know that if I chase long enough and hard enough, I am going to catch a big bite of that happiness."

The old alley cat reflected, "I have not been to cat philosophy school, but I know it is true that happiness is in the end of our tails. I have observed, however, that if I simply wander around enjoying my life, it follows me everywhere I go."

The way some of us run around in circles trying to be "productive" could be seen as trying to catch a big bite of that happiness somewhere outside ourselves. We could learn much from the wise old alley cat.

Actually, it is never *what* we do that matters, but why we do it, and how we feel as we achieve our results. When we are idle because we are happy and want to just enjoy life, we will find more happiness. When we are idle because we are unhappy, depressed, or bored, our discontent grows.

It is a popular opinion today that watching television is a waste of time. Maybe so, maybe not. We may

---

[1]Nightingale Conant Corp., The Human Resources Company, Chicago, Illinois.

watch television as part of our enjoyment of life, or as an effort to escape life. Or, we may avoid watching television because we are afraid of what other people will think, or because we have adopted the notion that only uneducated people who don't have anything better to do watch television.

The same could be said of any activity or inactivity in life. When achieving happiness and peace of mind is our only goal, we will know what to do regardless of what anyone else has ever thought or said.

THE ROAD TO HELL IS PAVED WITH GOOD INTENTIONS

Knowing that people have good intentions can inspire compassion instead of judgment. When good intentions fail, it is usually because thought-produced insecurities create detours.

We all have good intentions to be happy and do the best we can based on our present level of understanding. People who commit the most heinous crimes truly "know not what they do." They are deeply entrenched in a programmed thought system where *understanding* is beyond their reality.

Forgiveness is easy when we understand the good intentions of ourselves and others; it is difficult when we pay attention to the behavior resulting from the insecurities produced by a distorted thought system. The thought system distorts good intentions, and can interpret happiness as money, possessions, fame, power, or anything outside oneself.

People locked into their thought system and negative behavior create a kind of hell for themselves. It is our judgments of them that lead to our own kind of hell.

A PERSON WITHOUT GOALS IS LIKE A SHIP WITHOUT A RUDDER

A person with goals may in fact be like a boat—not without a rudder, but with a rudder stuck in one position. Being without goals allows us to enjoy opportunities as they come along. (Actually, goals from the heart will be much different from goals from the thought system.)

The belief that we must have goals often is based on thoughts that create insecurity, such as, "Without goals we will never accomplish anything." People who accomplish goals based on those thoughts do not accomplish happiness; instead, they feel only temporary satisfaction and quickly invent new goals.

When we are not focused on goals for the sake of ego reinforcement, we will see opportunities for the sake of enjoyment. Productivity is enhanced through enjoyment. With understanding, we want to accomplish only the things that are enhancing to ourselves and others, and we don't worry about satisfying our ego or other people's expectations.

New Year's resolutions so often fail after a brief spurt of success because it can take too much energy to satisfy the ego. So, many people give up. Success is effortless, however, when following inspiration from the heart.

176

We often look at someone who is accomplishing something and say, "Wow, she really has self-discipline and sticks to her goals." If you take a closer look, you may often find that she is following not a goal, but inspiration. Inspiration provides energy, whereas goals from the thought system drain energy. It is difficult not to follow inspiration, but it can be difficult to muster the energy to pursue goals from other sources.

Lest you start making it a rule not to have goals, when *understanding* takes you to your heart and inner wisdom, you may receive inspiration that leads you to a goal. As with everything else, goals are totally different when they come from the heart than when they come from a programmed thought system.

Deepak Chopra describes the difference between coming from the thought system and coming from the heart when he writes, "Learn to harness the power of intention, and you can create anything you desire. You can still get results through effort and through trying, but at a cost. The cost is stress, heart attacks, and the compromised function of your immune system."[2]

ANYTHING WORTH DOING
IS WORTH DOING WELL

The maxim "Anything worth doing is worth doing well" may be true if "well" simply means that you enjoy doing it; but "well" is usually a judgment, with

[2]Deepak Chopra, *The Seven Spiritual Laws of Success* (San Rafael: Amber-Allen Publishing & New World Library, 1994), pp. 75–76.

implications of perfection. Beliefs about perfection often take the joy out of doing.

How many people will not sing for the fun of it because they feel they cannot sing well enough? This is just one example of the many things people avoid doing for pleasure because they're afraid they won't live up to the judgment of doing it "well."

Anything worth doing is worth doing for the fun of it!

GROWTH IS PAINFUL

It is true that what is referred to as growth within the thought system is painful. Delving into the past for reasons or excuses, expressing feelings of anger based on blame, and controlling emotions are the kinds of growth that can be very painful. The pain is unnecessary.

Growth based on inspiration from your heart is not painful. It is painless to dismiss thoughts upon which the pain is based.

Healing programmed thoughts and beliefs is helpful only when it releases the pain and leaves room for love and compassion. We feel content when we see life with understanding, but it keeps getting better because our understanding continues to grow and deepen. There is nothing painful about it.

IT'S TOO GOOD TO BE TRUE

The only thing that can take away the goodness in something is negative thoughts. Think it, and you have it. If you think the goodness can't last, you have already started to create misery instead of enjoying what is.

If we think something can't last, it is because we have quit enjoying what is and have adopted thoughts such as, "I can't be happy if I don't have this," or, "It might not last," or, "I don't deserve it."

It is true that "it" might not last. So what? Becoming attached to it just keeps you from seeing so much more.

GOOD THINGS ALWAYS COME TO AN END

When we think, "Good things always come to an end," we have put on our blinders so we can't see the abundance of good things. Good things don't come to an end until we change our thoughts and start worrying about the past or future and stop enjoying *what is*. When we see the abundance of good things, it makes no sense to worry about losing one good thing.

From our heart, we will see what is with gratitude. There is always something to be grateful for.

Life is good.

15

Keys to Happiness: A Summary

Would you like to be in prison? Would you know-
ingly confine yourself to a life sentence in a dungeon? These questions may sound ridiculous at first,
but perhaps you have felt at times as though you've
locked yourself in a kind of prison without realizing
it. You may feel the confinement of the life you have
created without being aware that it is your creation.

Your thought system creates a prison as confin-
ing as any dungeon. The prison walls you create in
your mind are formed from illusionary thoughts, but
they can be as binding as concrete.

The foundation stones for a prison of illusions are
made of thoughts that create feelings of insecurity.
The walls are made of whatever form the insecurity
takes—self-importance, drinking, anxiety, overeating,

judgment, overachievement, expectations, stress, dis-satisfaction, depression, blame. The ceiling is the belief that these thoughts are reality.

THE PRINCIPLES AS KEYS TO HAPPINESS

An *understanding* of the principles we have dis-cussed in previous chapters is the master key to the prison doors. Know the truth, and the truth shall make you free.

There can be a wide chasm, however, between intellectual knowledge and experiential reality. Intel-lectually I believed that happiness came from within, but I did not understand the barriers that kept me from experiencing the truth of the knowledge. An *understanding* of the four principles provided the treasure map that led me past the barriers to my inner happiness. They are summarized here:

Thinking As a Function

The foundation principle is realizing that *thinking is a function*. This realization is the key to experiencing natural mental health and inner happiness. Those who believe wholly in the contents of their thinking often experience stress, anxiety, and other forms of insecurity. They take negative thoughts seriously, turn them into beliefs, and live for them. They have created perception prisons.

Those who understand that thinking is a function experience freedom and serenity. By seeing the humor in their negative creations and therefore not taking

182

them seriously, they are able to dismiss negativity and experience natural well-being from their heart or spiritual source. They have unlocked the prison doors.

Feelings As a Compass

The principle of *using our feelings as a compass* is the tool that lets us know where we are on our treasure map. Anytime we are feeling bad, we have forgotten that thinking is a function, and therefore we are seeing our thoughts as reality. Anytime we are feeling unconditional love, joy, gratitude, or compassion, the treasure is no longer buried; we are living from our heart and inner wisdom.

Separate Realities

When we understand the principle of *separate realities*, we see differences with interest and compassion rather than with judgment. Compassion does not mean we approve of every action by others; it means we understand their insecurity and lack of *understanding*. We often ignore the fact that we have made ourselves miserable with our judgments and forget that serenity is just a dropped thought away. When we see others with interest and compassion, it is because we are living from our heart.

Mood Levels

The principle of *mood levels*, or *levels of consciousness*, is closely related to the others. We are in a low mood

183

or level of consciousness when we forget that thinking is a function, when we forget to respect separate realities, when we forget to use our compass as a guide, and especially when we try to use our thought system to find a solution to our predicament. An *understanding* of this principle implies a higher level of consciousness, which will lead us to compassion for ourselves while we wait for a low mood to pass. Persistent low moods may be giving us the message that we need to seek help to heal troubling thoughts and beliefs from a deeply programmed thought system.

BARRIERS TO HAPPINESS

Between intellectual knowledge and experiential understanding of the principles, however, are barriers created in our thought system that can keep us from our inner happiness and serenity.

Circumstances

It is never the circumstances but our thoughts about them that create our state of mind. We can always find examples of people who have maintained their peace of mind under the very circumstances we think are causing us to feel awful, and many books have been written about their inspiring stories.

Refusing to understand this truth is what keeps people imprisoned in their judgments, in the hopelessness of victim mentality, and the bitterness of unforgiveness. A key to this prison door is to give up our belief that circumstances dictate our happiness, and to see that our serenity has everything to do with how we view circumstances.

Judgments

We judge others when we forget about separate realities, and delude ourselves that our reality is the right one. For everything we judge, someone else has been able to see the same event with compassion and understanding. Judgment is similar to the pot calling the kettle black, or "looking for the mote in the eye of another, when the beam in our own eye distorts our view."

When we observe others through our judgment filters, we are defining our own state of mind even while believing we are defining theirs. The person we are judging may be blinded by insecurity, taking some form of negativity, but if we were not blind ourselves, we would see the innocence and realize that person just doesn't know better. Instead of judgment we would feel compassion and understanding; we might then be inspired to do something to make that person feel more secure, or else stop judging and get out of the way.

A key that can release you from your judgments is to "look in the mirror." What "fault" of your own is reflected in your judgments? The prison door opens only when you see your own faults with compassion. What a gift it can be to see our own faults in others. What we might have been blind to before is seen clearly when we see it in others and acknowledge the reflection.

Expectations

When we are focused on expectations, we can be blind to the beauty and wonders right in front of us. Therefore, whenever we narrow our vision to expect certain outcomes, we greatly increase the probability of disappointment.

A key to happiness is to give up our expectations so we can see and enjoy *what is*. Remember. There are miracles all around us, in every moment. When living life from our heart, we *see* the miracles and are filled with gratitude.

Assumptions

Assuming that we know what someone else is thinking or experiencing is a mistake. We have missed a deep understanding of the principle of separate realities when we give credibility to our assumptions. When we base our thoughts and feelings on assumptions, we react to our assumptions and blame others for what we think they think. It can be humorous when we see it.

A loving mother relinquished custody of her children so they would not be torn apart in a court battle. She then assumed that people would judge her harshly and lived in fear of what others would think. Some did judge her harshly, but a majority of the people with whom she shared her experience reacted with compassion and statements of empathy: "That is the ultimate in unselfishness"; "What a sacrifice"; "That must have been a painful decision"; "You must really miss them." She finally realized that either she could tailor her life around her assumptions, and draw judgmental people into her life, or live from her heart and appreciate those who saw her circumstances with understanding.

A key to happiness is to give up our assumptions and live life freshly, moment to moment, from our heart and inner wisdom.

Beliefs and Realities

Alfred Adler once said, "Ideas have no meaning except the meaning we give them." We often attach such importance to the meaning we assign to our thoughts and ideas that they become beliefs we live and die for.

A firm belief in the flatness of the world does not make it so. Believing that because water is clear it is free of microorganisms doesn't mean they are not there.

A key to happiness is remembering that beliefs and realities are creations of our thoughts. Most of our thoughts were programmed when we couldn't see the truth, just as we can't see that the world is round. The truth that we find in our heart and inner wisdom can free us from the beliefs we created.

SIGNPOSTS TO HAPPINESS

Signposts on our treasure map provide keys to help us get past the barriers of our thought system to the experiential reality of our inner happiness and serenity.

Gratitude

Joe: "I can't see anything to be grateful for in this messed-up world."

Wise old Zeke: "I'll bet you would be a million-aire if I gave you $100 for everything you could think of to be grateful for."

You will see what you look for.

Gratitude is a natural feeling when negative thoughts have been dismissed. In higher levels of consciousness, we see the beauty of life that is all around us, and we are filled with gratitude. When we are grateful, we see how silly it is to be upset by some of the little things we take seriously in a lower state of mind.

When first learning about the principles, I felt disappointed in myself every time I got lost in thought. As my understanding increased, I stopped taking this seriously and had compassion for myself. Now I even feel a sense of gratitude when I get lost because I know I will come out of it with greater understanding. Every time I get off track and experience my judgments or any other form of negativity, the experience confirms that being lost in thought is not a pleasant place to be, and my understanding deepens.

It is impossible to feel gratitude and negativity at the same time. My understanding of that truth lets me know that it makes sense to focus on what I am grateful for, rather than on what I have been thinking about to make myself unhappy.

Gratitude is my favorite key.

Compassion

Feeling compassion is another natural occurrence when we see what thought is. With perspective, we see the innocence in others and know that they do the very best they can from their present level of understanding.

A key to happiness is allowing ourselves to experience the compassion from our heart that makes it easy to forgive ourselves as well as others.

What We See (or Feel or Give) Is What We Get

When we are in a low mood and feeling judgmental or angry, we are stuck with those feelings. When we are in a high mood and see the innocence of all behavior, we have feelings of love, compassion, and understanding; we have peace of mind. When we give love, that is what we get. We don't have to get it from someone else, because love is inherent in the feelings we have when we give love.

A key to happiness is understanding that we reap what we sow.

Love and Understanding

The greatest key of all is love. When we feel loving, we see beauty and goodness in everything—or at least, we see the perfection of all things. All that is needed to solve any problem we can imagine is love.

Love and understanding are the same thing. Love without understanding is conditional (not love at all). With understanding, it is impossible to judge; with understanding, we have compassion; with understanding, we have peace of mind and contentment; with understanding, we have love.

Remember that understanding is not about shoulds. Suppose you don't feel loving—so what?

You feel what you feel, based on your present level of understanding. "Shoulding" yourself about that just makes it worse. Understanding usually changes what you feel, but if you try to change it through shoulds, you block understanding.

A key to happiness is listening to your inner wisdom until understanding sneaks past your thought system.

The Battle Between Love and Ego

Love is the ultimate reality; ego is the ultimate illusion. Ego is the need to prove self-importance, which is based on the illusory belief in insecurity. It is the source of jealousy, self-righteousness, possessiveness, judgment, expectation, revenge, depression, stress, and disease.

What power this illusion of ego can create.

But love has a greater power: Love heals every problem. Through the perspective of love, problems disappear. Love fills us with feelings that guide us to solutions that make the problem seem insignificant.

Joe chided Zeke, "All this talk of love sounds like religion and the flower children from the sixties to me. It really turns me off."

Wise old Zeke replied, "Could it be that the reason you don't have much love in your life is because it turns you off?"

A key to happiness is recognizing the difference between love and ego so that ego can be dismissed and love can be enjoyed.

Enjoying What Is *While It Is*

Have you ever looked back at a time in your life and thought, "I was really happy then. Too bad I didn't appreciate it more at the time." Have you known others who thought their circumstances were a tragedy, but later saw them as the best thing that ever happened to them? This is an example of the perfection of all things. We may not be able to understand the perfection at the moment, unless we have understanding.

When we understand the principles, the beauty of life is profound. What used to seem ordinary or insignificant is seen with appreciation and gratitude. We are often so filled with beauty, contentment, and the wonder of life that we have no choice except to get quiet and enjoy it.

A key to happiness is to enjoy what is.

Happiness and Serenity

What could be more important than happiness and serenity? When happiness is what we want, it makes no sense to entertain thoughts that lead in any other direction

Can you imagine the wonderful revolution that will take place when we all start dismissing the many thoughts that create so much misery?

This key to happiness is so simple. Dismiss negative thoughts and you have happiness and serenity.

As a man thinketh, so is he.

Index

Confusion, 76
Controlling behavior, 62
Cooling-off periods, 162–163
Coping skills, 5–6
Counting to ten, 170
*A Course in Miracles: Work-
    book for Students,* 132
Cults, 124

D

Decision-making, 113–115
Deepening under-
    standing, 77
Defense mechanisms, 88
Depression, 5
    cycles of, 54–55
    thinking and, 17–18
Detours, 123–140
    avoidance of, 139–140
Difference, enjoyment
    of, 49
Dismissing negative
    thoughts, 36–37
Dissatisfaction, 112–113
Doing, 109–110
Drug use, 1
Dyer, Wayne, 16, 27,
    33–34, 174

E

Edison, Thomas, 69
Ego, 16
    forgiveness and, 117
    goals and, 176
    gratification, 13

love and, 190
    self-importance and,
        124–126
Emotions, thinking and, 23
Enjoyment of what is, 191
Expectations, 102
    as barrier to happi-
        ness, 185
    doing and, 110
    living up to, 129–130

F

Factual information, 21
Failure, sense of, 172
False needs, 7
Feelings compass,
    31–41, 183
    anger and, 33, 72–73, 82
    chart of, 37–39
    as guide, 74–75
    separate realities, 51
Fighting in relationships,
    163–164
Forgetting, forgiveness and,
    117–118
Forgiveness, 11, 38,
    117–118
    anger and, 135
    good intentions and, 175
Fun in relationships, 153

G

Generation gaps, 44
Gifts from Eykis (Dyer), 27
Gifts in all things, 103

FOR MORE INFORMATION

Jane Nelsen shares her wealth of information in workshops and lectures throughout the world.

Topics include:

Understanding: Eliminating Stress and Finding Serenity in Life and Relationships
Positive Discipline in the Classroom
Teaching Parenting the Positive Discipline Way
(This workshop is designed for facilitator training for parent educators, and may have a specific focus for parents of preschoolers, parents of teenagers, parents of children ages six to twelve, or parents in recovery.)

Workshops, lectures and facilitator trainings are scheduled throughout the United States each year. Dates and locations are available by contacting:

Empowering People Associates
P.O. Box 788
Fair Oaks, CA 95628
916-961-5551 • Fax: 916-961-5570

For a free newsletter, contact:
Empowering People Books, Tapes & Videos
P.O. Box 1926
Orem, UT 84059
1-800-456-7770

ORDER FORM

To: Empowering People, P.O. Box 1926, Orem, UT 84059
Phone: 1-800-456-7770 (credit card orders only)   Fax: 801/726-0022

	Price	Quantity	Amount
BOOKS			
Understanding: Eliminating Stress... by Nelsen	$12.00	_____	_____
Raising Self-Reliant Children in a Self-Indulgent			
World by Glenn & Nelsen	$12.95	_____	_____
Positive Discipline A-Z by Nelsen, Lott & Glenn	$14.95	_____	_____
Positive Discipline in the Classroom by Nelsen, Lott &			
Glenn	$14.95	_____	_____
Positive Discipline: A Teacher's A-Z Guide by			
Nelsen, Duffy, Escobar, Ortolano & Owen-Sohocki	$14.95	_____	_____
Positive Discipline for Teenagers by Nelsen & Lott	$14.95	_____	_____
Positive Discipline by Nelsen	$11.00	_____	_____
Positive Discipline for Single Parents by Nelsen,			
Erwin & Delzer	$12.95	_____	_____
Positive Discipline for Preschoolers by Nelsen,			
Erwin & Duffy	$14.00	_____	_____
Time Out: Abuses & Effective Uses by Nelsen & Glenn	$6.95	_____	_____
Positive Discipline for Parenting in Recovery			
by Nelsen, Intner & Lott	$12.95	_____	_____
The Family That Works Together... by Lott & Intner	$9.95	_____	_____
To Know Me Is To Love Me by Lott, Kentz & West	$10.00	_____	_____
Together and Liking It by Lott and West	$7.95	_____	_____
TAPES & VIDEOS			
Positive Discipline cassette tape	$10.00	_____	_____
Positive Discipline video	$49.95	_____	_____
Building Healthy Self-Esteem through Positive			
Discipline by Nelsen	$10.00	_____	_____
Positive Discipline in the Classroom cassette tapes	$49.95	_____	_____
Positive Discipline in the Classroom video	$9.95	_____	_____
MANUALS			
Teaching Parenting the Positive Discipline Way	$39.95	_____	_____
Positive Discipline for Parenting in Recovery	$19.95	_____	_____
Positive Discipline for Single Parents	$19.95	_____	_____
Positive Discipline for Preschoolers	$19.95	_____	_____
Positive Discipline in the Classroom	$39.95	_____	_____
Student Assistance through Positive Discipline	$19.95	_____	_____

SUBTOTAL _____

Sales tax: UT add 6.25%;   CA add 7.25%   _____

Shipping & Handling: $2.50 plus 50¢ for each item   _____

TOTAL _____

(Prices subject to change without notice.)

METHOD OF PAYMENT (check one):
_____ Check made payable to Empowering People Books, Tapes & Videos
_____ Mastercard, Visa, Discover Card, American Expess

Card #_____ Expiration _____/_____
Ship to_____
Address_____
City/State/Zip_____
Daytime Phone_____